SUNBURSTS

True Adventures of
Toccoa Falls College Missionaries

Compiled and Edited by
LORENE MOOTHART, A.B., M.A.

Illustrated by Cynthia Poser

Copyright © 1992 by Toccoa Falls College

ACKNOWLEDGMENTS

Song "Into My Heart," Author Harry Clarke, copyright © 1924, renewal 1952, Hope Publishing Company. Used by permission.

Testimony of David Guzman, "From Books to the Book," (in the article "God Raised up a Lazarus," by Ruth Good), *Alliance Life*, July 7, 1970. Used by permission.

Article "A Race with Time for the Jarai New Testament and Psalms" used by special permission of the author Charles Long.

Romans 8:37-39--Taken from the New American Standard Bible, copyright © 1960, 1962, 1963, 1968, 1971, 1972, 1973, 1975, 1977 by the Lockman Foundation. Used by permission.

Matthew 28:20b--Copyright © J.B. Phillips, 1959, 1960, 1972. Used by permission.

John 17:24--From the HOLY BIBLE, NEW INTERNATIONAL VERSION. Copyright © 1973, 1978, 1984 International Bible Society. Used by permission of Zondervan Publishing House. All rights reserved.

All other scripture references are taken from the King James Version of the Bible.

Printed by Toccoa Falls Press

DEDICATION

"I thank God for Toccoa Falls College where I got the grounding in the Word of God and the teaching of the Scriptures, and I thank God for those professors and teachers and dorm parents who loved us and cared for us and helped us." --C.G. Ingram

"I came to TFI as a very new Christian; I knew very little about the Bible or how to live the Christian life. At TFI I learned much and I learned it well. God graciously gave me good instruction in the faith." --John Cook

"Many years later (after working my way through high school and college at TFI), I knew it was the faculty and staff who made the greatest sacrifice. We were the products of the most dedicated faculty in the world." --George Henderson

It is to these, the faculty and staff of Toccoa Falls College, both past and present, devoted servants of Christ, sacrificial laborers, loving examples, that this book is reverently dedicated.

FOREWORD

Miss Moothart is a very interesting person. She served as a faculty member under Dr. Richard A. Forrest and wrote his biography, *Achieving the Impossible--With God*. That book, now in its fourth printing, is still blessing literally thousands of people.

She has produced another book that I believe is going to bring real joy and blessing to thousands more. This new book containing graphic illustrations of exploits of Toccoa Falls alumni will be a great inspiration to young people, to continue obeying the Master's call to the regions beyond.

Miss Moothart, after serving here at Toccoa Falls College, went to Ohio and taught in the public school system. Then upon retirement she fulfilled a lifetime desire; she was appointed as a missionary associate to teach in the Alliance Academy in Quito, Ecuador. She has since returned to Toccoa Falls College. This book is the culmination of years of plans to record the activities of some of God's servants from TFC who minister around the world. I believe it will be a great blessing to all who read it, particularly to alumni of this fine institution.

This book is a tribute to those who have taught here at Toccoa Falls College in years past. It is also a tribute to those who have obeyed the Lord and done exploits for Him around the world. Included are experiences from just a small number of those graduates who have served at home and abroad for our Coming King. Many intriguing real-life incidents are told here, as well as humorous happenings. But the glorious victories related will encourage us all, whatever our task may be.

The college continues to train young men and women who answer His call to service overseas. One of the choice majors on this campus today continues to be World Mission.

> Dr. Paul L. Alford, President
> Toccoa Falls College

PREFACE

SUNBURST--"A flash of light through a break in the clouds." Is this not an exemplification of the life of each missionary: a flash of spiritual life through a break in the clouds of darkness he encounters as he ministers day by day on the mission field?

It was the desire of Dr. and Mrs. Forrest to serve on the mission field; instead, God called them to establish Toccoa Falls College, and in so doing to multiply themselves on the field through the many students of the school who have been called to become "flashes of light" in far-off places. In a sense, *SUNBURSTS* could be considered a sequel to *Achieving the Impossible--With God,* the continuation of the work begun those many years ago.

Despite their busy, often hectic, schedules, a number of missionaries and former missionaries have contributed from their experiences in order that the reader may get a glimpse into life in a foreign country as God's representative. The book should acquaint the reader more intimately with life on the field, encourage him in his own life and in his prayer life as he lifts the missionaries to the Lord, and show him how vital is the work of missions. Actually, the sole purpose of the book is to glorify God, to show His love, His faithfulness, His help, His guidance, and His joy as the missionary "breaks through the clouds of sin" in far-flung regions of the earth.

The missionaries whose stories are included herein are only a representative few of those who have gone out from Toccoa Falls College; many others could not be contacted for various reasons, but all have helped to further the cause of Christ! Praise His Name!

May I express my sincere thanks to all those who have encouraged me in the compiling and editing of this book, as well as to those who have contributed. Especially I wish to thank Mrs. James (Suzanne) Rich for proofreading the manuscript and making valuable suggestions, to Mrs. Ed (Cynthia) Poser for designing the cover and making the superb pen-and-ink sketches which appear throughout the book, and to Miss Brenda Ritchey and the print shop staff, who so cheerfully added the printing of this book to their already heavy schedule of work.

May *SUNBURSTS* be a blessing to each one who reads it!

SUNBURSTS

"Flashes of light through breaks in the clouds"

FROM TOCCOA FALLS
CALL AND PREPARATION
"Anything, Lord, But . . . "	George Henderson	13
Is God Big Enough?	Clair Black	17
To Go or Not to Go	Patricia Brown	20

TO THE WORLD
AFRICA
The British Cameroons
The Ultimate Service	Alma Henderson	27
Susanna Taught the Missionary	Alma Henderson	33

Burkina Faso
A Calling Card in Bobo-Dioulasso
                              Michelle Tatum Stanford   37

Côte d'Ivoire
On the Last Day!	Jean Hotalen	39
William, Moussa, and Ron	Donald O. Young	44

Gabon
Miracle in an African Night	Anita Reader	49
Blessings Immeasurable	Clarence Walker	53

Mali
Be Ready to Preach, Pray, or Die   Doloris Burns Bandy   57

Nigeria
Contrasts: Light and Darkness   Goldie Blakeney   62

Sudan, Dinkaland
Sowing for Christ in Dinkaland	Travis McDonald	68
Our Heathen Sisters in Dinkaland	Evelyn McDonald	74

ASIA
India
Two Thankful Lepers   Ferne Gerrie   81

Korea
Camp Mount O Pines   John Cook   87

Malaysia
  More Than Conqueror   Rebecca Carter Egeler   90

Thailand
  Even to the Smallest Detail   Deborah Eckman   95

Viet Nam
  YaHa, Prince Among Men   C.G. Ingram   99
  With the Katu in Viet Nam   LeRoy Josephsen   104
  A Race with Time for the Jarai
    New Testament and Psalms   Charles Long   110

THE ISLAND COUNTRIES
Indonesia
  From the Other Side of the World   Judy Gaskin   119

Irian Jaya
  "Before They Call, I Will Answer"   Carolyn Eckman   121
  Ihu Mauri's Requests and Praises   Carolyn Eckman   125
  Attending a Cannibal Feast   Frances Bozeman   128
  The Gospel Invades the Baliem Valley   James Sunda   131

Japan
  Sharing the Word with Russian Seamen   Sue Benedict   138
  Determining to Triumph   Georgalyn Wilkinson   143

New Zealand
  Debbie Gibson, Our First Adult Convert
                                      Richard Applegate   148

Papua New Guinea
  God's Faithfulness in Papua New Guinea   Mark Hepner   152

LATIN AMERICA
Brazil
  God's Great Goodness   Ann Hemminger   159

Chile
  Buckets of Dirty Water   Patricia Hall   163
  Radio HOPE--A Series of Miracles   Raymond Woerner   167

Colombia
  Endeavoring to Hold a Street Meeting in Bogota
                                            Steve Irvin   173
  God Holds Up a Fiesta   David Overmoyer   176

Ecuador
The Alliance Academy
  The Fifth-Graders' Secret   Milton Brown   179

God's Sufficiency	Terrilynn Kadle	183
God Healed Our Son Through Prayer	John Rollins	187
The Field Ministry		
Genuine Faith	John McCarthy	191
Planting the Batan Church	Milton Brown	193
"What Do You Think About Good Witches?"	Connie Smith	197
Munca and His Two Wives	David Miller	200

Mexico

God Overrules the Power of Man	Ramon Esparza	203

Peru

God Raised Up a "Lazarus"	Ruth Good	206

ELSEWHERE

Alaska

"He Goeth Before"	Louise Couchey	213

England

A Wrong Turn--with a Right Ending	Michelle Tatum Stanford	218

Jordan

Fantastic Was the Week in Jordan	Norman Allison	220
Under Fire in Amman, Jordan	Norman Allison	224

FROM TOCCOA FALLS

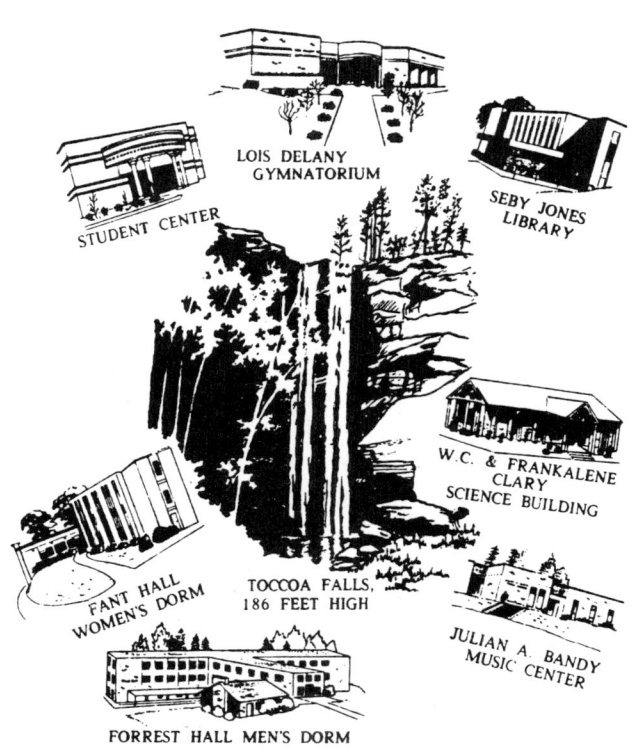

Call and Preparation

ALMA MATER

Toccoa Falls, the beautiful,
   With mount and vale so fair;
Our Institute more blessed still,
   In truth and holy prayer.

Our students come from near and far
   Thy knowledge to receive
In ancient lore and culture true,
   And God's own Word believe.

Our students go to far-off lands,
   Where sin and darkness bind;
To free men's souls from bondage drear,
   And give light to the blind.

CHORUS

Toccoa Falls, thy name we love,
   We pray God's power on thee;
God keep thee faithful to thy task;
   God keep thee pure and free.

                     --Dr. George Shaw

The Call

"ANYTHING, LORD, BUT . . . "

GEORGE HENDERSON

George Henderson was a Toccoa Falls College senior when he had to answer the most important questions in his life: "Are you fully committed? Will you go?"

"Our students go to far-off lands where sin and darkness bind." So goes the song of our Alma Mater at Toccoa Falls College, written by Dr. George Shaw, our beloved teacher who taught us so much in word and deed.

Through the years, hundreds of students have lustily sung those words, and many have made the commitment to be part of that train of students to fulfil the great commission of Jesus Christ to carry the Gospel to the ends of the earth. We were often reminded in chapel: "The sun never sets on the witness of Toccoa Falls students who have gone to carry the Gospel around the world." It was thrilling to be part of such a noble family of stalwarts.

But how does that call "to go to far-off lands" come? Who is to go? Which students? What students will make the sacrifice? To whom will the Lord give this privilege? Every serious Bible student is at some time confronted with these questions. "Who . . . ME?"

Time and again I had made a commitment to Jesus Christ. For this reason I had come to Toccoa Falls in 1938, penniless, naive, green as grass, but with a will to prepare to serve my Lord. As Dr. Forrest said, "Every student who is willing to work will be given an opportunity to prepare"; so I worked my way through eight years of high school and college. Such was the lot of the majority of students during the Great Depression. Many years later, I knew it was the faculty and staff who made the greatest sacrifice. We were the products of the most dedicated faculty in the world.

In 1946, when I was a senior in college, I had the privilege to be the student pastor of a Baptist church in the North Georgia mountains. Since it was adjacent to a large secular boarding school, many of the students there attended our church. During a series of evangelistic meetings near the end of the school year, we tried to challenge those students to a life of dedication to our Lord. There was *no* response! Why?

It was on my knees at night in the office of the LeTourneau Company, where I had become the night personnel manager, that the question of "Why?" was answered.

I had repeatedly told the Lord that I was willing to do anything He asked me to do . . . except . . . perhaps . . . "to go to far-off lands where sin and darkness bind." I didn't consider myself "missionary material." I was not "the type" of person that would make a "good missionary." My aesthetic sense abhorred dirt and grime, disease and pain, misery and suffering. Most of the missionary accounts I had heard from the pioneers involved a daily routine of this. I told myself I couldn't possibly be a candidate.

I knew that night alone in my office the reason that the young people of my church were not responding to a life of dedication to Jesus. Their pastor himself, who gave the invitation, had never completely made that commitment. That night on his knees the pastor responded unreservedly, honestly, and completely to "'go where You want me to go, dear Lord . . . be what You want me to be.' I'll even be willing to 'go to far-off lands where sin and darkness bind.'" When the pastor responded to the invitation of consecration, the students responded. More than twenty were baptized in the school swimming pool during the succeeding week. Now the major problem was settled. Where would God lead? What would God do?

A tall, blond young lady with a vivacious personality and abundant energy to match, who knew what she would do with her life and where she must go, had graduated in my senior class just two weeks previously. She had repeatedly injected into every conversation and public testimony the need for missionaries to serve in Africa, and she particularly stressed the shortage of men applying to the mission. I remembered squirming during one speech she gave in class, wondering when she'd ever finish. Her enthusiasm and excitement over the prospect of going to Africa "bugged" me. She had already made all the decisions that I had yet to face. I had to find her for some answers to my questions.

The rest of that love story is history. We were commissioned as missionaries in August, 1946, in Tacoma, Washington, to go to the Cameroons of West Africa, where we served for twenty-two years.

Now, almost a half century later, I am amazed at the gracious invitation of our Lord to a life of commitment that He gives to His children, and I am equally amazed at the beggarly response that His children often give to that invitation. To think that by an act of my will, I might have turned away the greatest privilege that can ever come to a human being, to speak the words of Life to those who have never heard, just baffles the mind. To know that some soul who had never heard but by my going will greet me in heaven because of my obedience gives inner joy and anticipation to this aging soul.

I am thankful to the Lord that He kept on calling and that eventually I responded. Oh, the love and patience of our God, and the grace that brought it down to man, that we can be His hands and feet, and His mouthpiece to share this life-giving message to the whole world!

The Call

IS GOD BIG ENOUGH?

CLAIR BLACK

Clair and Elizabeth Black have served as missionaries of the C&MA in Indonesia since 1981. During the 1990-1991 school year, he was the Missionary-in-Residence at Toccoa Falls College, after which they returned to Enarotali, Irian Jaya.

When I was in high school I felt strongly that I should go to Bible school. I didn't want to because I didn't like school. I didn't like to study; I didn't like to write. I enjoyed woodshop and metal shop and gym class, as well as other classes where I didn't have a lot of reading and writing to do.

However, the feeling that I should go to college would not leave; instead, it became a conviction. I knew that God wanted me to become a missionary; I accepted the challenge. I didn't know how God was going to lead me to a Bible school, but felt that He was going to help me.

Finally I went to my counselor and stated, "I'm going to college; I'm going to a Bible college. I'm going to be a minister or a missionary."

My counselor looked at my records, then he looked at me and with a sigh answered, "Son, you're not college material."

Nevertheless, I enrolled at Toccoa Falls College, and within a couple of weeks I realized I *wasn't* college material. I was glad to see how the Lord had helped me: I wasn't college material; yet the Lord enabled me to complete the first step toward the mission field.

In Bible school, since I was planning to become a missionary, I had to take a language aptitude test. It had something to do with studying letters and spelling and their sounds. Needless to say, I did not do a very good job on the test. As a matter of fact, I was never told the results. The only time you're told your score is if you're very good. Then the professors say, "Why don't you become a missionary; you're going to be good at learning another language."

They did not tell me that. They told Elizabeth, my wife--she did very well. Despite this seeming hindrance, I still felt that God wanted me on the mission field.

Two years later I received my second college degree--this time from the Canadian Theological College. Then Elizabeth and I took a pastorate for three years. After that, we went to Toronto Institute of Linguistics, where we took a thirty-day course of intensive training in how to learn a foreign language. At the close of the program, when your final paper is graded and returned, you find at the bottom of the page the word "Matched" or "Unmatched" regarding the country for which you're suited. You'll never guess what I had. That's right: "Unmatched."

That day the Institute reported to the Christian and Missionary Alliance in Nyack, New York, that this candidate was not qualified to go as a missionary; he could not learn a second language. It didn't sound very good. Still, I continued to feel that God wanted me on the mission field. Evidently the powers-that-be at Headquarters thought, "Let's give it a try anyhow; what can we lose?" ($25,000 a year then!)

They sent us, not on the special capacity I had, but on the ability that Elizabeth showed, probably figuring that if I got malaria and died, they'd still have her. We were assigned to Irian Jaya, and when the executive committee members there read our records, I imagine they thought, "What have we here? This fellow cannot learn two more languages, so let's put him at Nabire where we'll see if he can learn one."

We went to Nabire, where a first-termer is not allowed to go home on his first furlough until he has learned the language, or when he does leave, he is not allowed to return. Well, I give the glory to God; we were invited back. We did learn the language that God provided for us. Not only that, but the last year of our second term we were transferred inland to Enarotali, where we shall begin to learn the dialect that is spoken there!

I want you to know that God will provide for you and for me for our special needs, whatever they are. If God has given you a job to do, if God has called you to a particular area or certain ministry, God is going to help you through.

Yes, God is *always* big enough!

The Call

TO GO OR NOT TO GO

PATRICIA BROWN

Milton and Pat Brown have served in Ecuador since 1963, eighteen of those years as dorm parents at The Alliance Academy in Quito. Currently they are missionaries to the youth in the Batan Church there. Milton is also the field director of Ecuador.

During our last interview with the Mission Board before we left for Costa Rica for language study in 1963, Milton and I were asked what we would like to do as missionaries. Milton replied, "I am prepared to preach . . . and if there should ever be a need for dorm parents, we would like to do that." (He had had a positive experience as assistant to dorm parents, Bill and Mary Kadle, in a high school boys' dorm at Toccoa Falls when he was a student in the college.)

While we were in Costa Rica, there arose an urgent need for dorm parents in Quito at The Alliance Academy. Milton wrote our Field Chairman, Henry Miller, to tell him we would be willing to be dorm parents. Henry wrote back saying in effect, "Thanks, but no, thanks." He expressed the importance of our getting a good foundation in Spanish and being involved in field ministries at least the first term, before thinking about being dorm parents.

During our days of orientation upon our arrival in Quito, Chairman Miller had taken us on a tour through The Alliance Academy and through the dorm. As we saw the magnitude of that job, I verbally expressed my feelings, "This is one job I would never be able to do." We would have to supply as substitute parents, working with children, making up to them the lack of being home with their parents, and helping them to increase their love and respect for their parents. They weren't here at the school because the parents wanted them out of their way so they could do missionary work. These kids came because their parents were serving the Lord and there wasn't a proper education in the countries and places where the parents were serving. I did not feel qualified for this tremendous task.

Two years later, after serving as pastor and wife in a Spanish church in Latacunga, Ecuador, and shortly after the birth of our first child, we *were* asked to be dorm parents. A crisis had come; there was a critical need for dorm parents in the Academy. Milton's first reaction was an overwhelming "Yes!" Mine was pure hesitation. I had always loved younger children: older young people frightened me!

As we talked and prayed, Milton suggested that I seek the Lord for a special verse concerning this situation, as has been my system during all my Christian life. I laughingly replied, "If the Lord will give me a verse with the words 'young people' in it, I will go to the dorm."

I dedicated myself to seeking the Lord's will, for it was no laughing matter, really. I knew that if Milton made the decision to go to the dorm, I would follow him. After all, had I not said Ruth's vows to Milton during our wedding ceremony? "Whither thou goest, I will go. . . . " At the same time I needed assurance for *myself* from the Lord *Himself.*

As I was reading in my daily devotional time, I found myself in the Psalms. When I came to Psalm 127:3 and read, "Lo, children are an heritage of the Lord," I felt as though I was getting "warm" but when I read verse four, I knew that this was the Lord's call: "As arrows are in the hand of a mighty man; so are the children of the YOUTH." I had asked for "young people" and I do not know of a verse in the King James Bible (the only one used in those days) with "young people" in it, but here was the word "youth." Psalm 128:3 further confirmed the Lord's voice to me: "Thy wife shall be as a fruitful vine by the sides of thine house; thy children like olive plants round about thy table."

We went to the dorm in July 1966 for one year . . . and ended up staying a total of eighteen years, taking care of 150 different boys and girls ages 6-18 during those years. Three times a day "our" children were like olive plants round about our table. The Lord never once failed us, and we are so thankful for His faithfulness to us and to the children of our missionary families throughout South America. I wouldn't trade those years for anything. If I had to make the decision again to go or not to go to the dorm, I would *go!*

TO THE WORLD

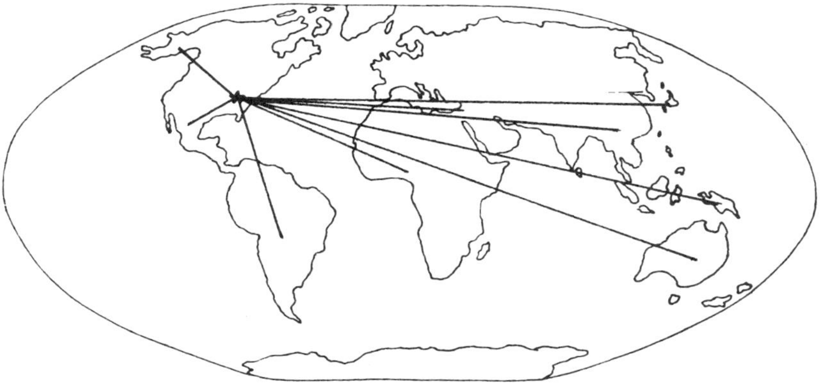

AFRICA

The British Cameroons

THE ULTIMATE SERVICE

ALMA HENDERSON

George and Alma Henderson went to the British Cameroons of Africa in 1947 under the auspices of the Cameroon Baptist Missions. George is also an artist and after returning to the States, has taught art in the University of Georgia in Athens.

What is the ultimate service that a foreign missionary can render to prove his love for the people to whom he has come to minister? It took me twenty years to find out. . . .

When we went to the British Cameroons as missionaries and began the task of sharing God's love with a foreign people who had a foreign language and a culture we had not learned to understand, the prospects seemed bleak. Missionaries had gone before us, and their gravestones were evidence of their dedication. We faced a battle against principalities and powers and the rulers of this dark world.

Our first assignment was to open a mission station on the coast, where churches, though existent, were weak and often divided.

As we gathered the Christians together and prayed for God's direction, the people responded. After securing land from the local chief and town council, we began the process of uniting the Christians to build: clear the jungle, get sand from the river bottoms, gather stones, dig foundations, and cut timbers in the forests. One after another, the structures arose. It took leadership, not just a little energy, lots of sweat, and, most of all, a vision to see the church of Jesus Christ established. Today a Christian school, a Christian college, and a church stand on that plot.

Our second assignment sent us inland to open a new mission station in a jungle area with dense growth where the tsetse and crysop flies flourished; disease was prevalent; dysentery and tropical fevers claimed countless lives. A fertile area where many people from the hinterlands came to settle, it was a stronghold of ju-ju (animism) and many pagan practices. Here we felt the Gospel must gain entrance and be established.

Again we gathered the handful of Christians together in their tiny thatched church, prayed and sought direction from God, and together we searched the scriptures and prayed until the Christians caught the vision of building a permanent structure for God.

The most prominent hill in the area was secured from the local chief. Again the bush had to be cleared and a road built by hand to the top of the hill--headpan by headpan;

then the stones were gathered and sand was carried by headpan from the river. Bricks had to be made, one by one.

As Christians worked, everyone in the village watched the process. *What is going on on that hill?* From afar one could see the Christians working. But why on that high hill? *Those foolish Christians expending all that energy when they might have built at the foot of the hill and saved all that effort!*

The Christians, however, knew their strategy. They had learned Jesus' words: "You are the light of the world. A city set on a hill cannot be hidden . . . In the same way, let your light shine before men that they may see your good deeds, and praise your Father in heaven."

Finally the church was completed. It could be seen from far and wide, with the cross of Jesus Christ towering over the whole community. When dedication day arrived, the crowds came by the hundreds and filled the whole hillside; even the Moslem chief and his entourage came and sat on the front seat to listen, to look, to wonder. What had this handful of Christians done, and what will they yet do?

The greatest need for spreading the Gospel is a strong native spiritual leadership. The need was desperate. Like the early church, we needed godly leaders like Stephen, Timothy, Barnabas, and Silas.

God is faithful. From His own native sons, He raised up one named Daniel Moky and called him to proclaim the Good News to his people. Daniel was obedient to that call. He attended our Mission Bible School, then came back to Kumba field with a burning desire to carry the Gospel to the villages hidden in the forests, nestled beside the rivers, and dwelling across the mountains.

For years with Pastor Moky we trekked over those

Barombi steeps and forded the rushing streams, visiting the small villages hidden in the jungles--preaching, teaching, evangelizing, and baptizing new believers. Pastor Moky was faithful in planting the Gospel seed throughout that area and rejoiced over the seed that fell on fertile soil and sprouted and brought forth fruit.

One week during the heavy rainy season, Pastor Moky and George decided to go to baptize some new believers in a distant village behind Cameroon Mountain, visiting some of the small churches along the way. Meanwhile, I went with a gospel team of women to visit the churches in the mangrove swamps, where transportation would be by canoe.

My group and I had a wonderful time in the fishing villages, sharing our testimonies, gathering the children for Bible stories, and teaching the women God's standard for godly womanhood. The women could be heard for miles up the creeks as they sang and sang while the canoes ferried us from village to village. The fellowship was sweet, and the women grew stronger as they learned to speak unashamedly about their faith in Christ.

* * * * * * *

When I returned to the mission station in Kumba, I knew something was wrong. A sinister silence had fallen over the whole town, and the mission station itself had an eerie quietness hovering over it. I could feel it in the air. *What was the matter?*

Seeing me, the headmistress of our school came running to tell me the news: Pastor Moky had died and had been buried while I was away!

It couldn't be! He had been here the day I left, robust and full of energy and enthusiasm. He was going to baptize believers. What had happened?

When? Where? How?

Clara poured forth the story. Pastor Moky had come home from the trek with a strangulated hernia. They came late at night to the mission station, and George took him to the hospital and gave instructions there that Pastor Moky must see a doctor immediately. Whatever the cost, George would see that it was paid.

"I must leave at once for another village, but I'll be back in a few days. Above all, take care of Pastor Moky." And George was gone.

Pastor Moky lay in the government hospital three days in desperate pain, without seeing a doctor or receiving treatment of any kind. His was death by neglect, as happens so often in Africa. The whole community was shocked, angry, hurt, brokenhearted. Their spiritual leader was dead, a prince among men! What would they do now?

By this time a host of Christians had gathered on the mission veranda to share the sad tidings. They wept intermittently as they poured out their hearts.

"If only I had been home, I might have helped in some way," I stammered.

"No, Nyango, there is nothing you could have added to the 'wonderful thing' that Songo did. The whole village is talking about it. He will always be remembered for this 'wonderful thing.' You could not have added anything more. WE DIDN'T NEED YOU!"

Those words were like a sharp arrow. I thought I was always needed. Could not I have helped in some way to ease their troubled hearts? Like a broken record they repeated *the wonderful thing that Songo did*.

Finally I asked, "What is this wonderful thing that Songo did?" I don't think that even George knew the answer.

Our headmistress explained. When Pastor Moky died, George went to his little thatched house in the middle of the village, and, since it was the custom for the nearest member of the family to prepare the body for burial, George took it upon himself to wash the body of his brother in Christ and to dress him for burial.

"No one has ever seen a white man wash and dress one of our dead bodies . . . and he stayed there . . . and the people saw him weep." This was to them the ultimate service of love. Suddenly I realized what was important, *the test of love!*

Acquiring land and clearing the bush for new mission stations may be time-consuming and difficult, but it isn't the acid test. Gathering stones and sand and making bricks for the erection of churches and buildings may be necessary, trekking over hills in the heat of the tropical sun may be tiresome and exhausting, and preaching and teaching is needful, but they too may fail the test.

Here, unbeknown to himself, George had passed the test. The people had seen the missionary identify with a brother in the most loving way that is known to these people, *and nothing more was needed!* That one act had been greater than anything else he had done in twenty years.

Then I remembered the scripture about Lazarus: "Jesus wept. The Jews said, 'See how He loved him'" (John 11:35, 36). "I have set you an example," Jesus said, "do as I have done" (John 13:15).

This is the ultimate test of the service of love!

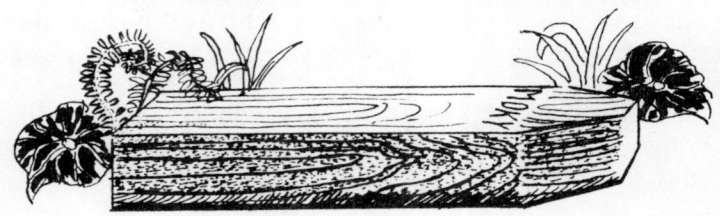

The British Cameroons

SUSANNA TAUGHT THE MISSIONARY

ALMA HENDERSON

As Alma Henderson has depicted the ultimate service of the missionary to the nationals of the British Cameroons, so she now relates how love was shown by a national to the missionary.

A dear soul named Susanna was a childless widow in the British Cameroons, a land where being childless is like having a dreaded plague. Although she had borne eight children, all had died and left her alone in a cruel world. Perhaps this was one of the reasons she was drawn to our Christian meetings. Here she found comfort and hope in the midst of her dreary surroundings. Susanna was totally illiterate, but she clung tenaciously to the words of Jesus that she heard--as a pearl clings to an oyster. Although a wide gulf of difference separated us, we soon became fast friends. She shared her joys and woes with me, and always in our Lord she found a solution.

The time had come for our furlough, and, as always, we discarded our old clothes that had gone through more than three-and-a-half years of hard wear and washing. Much of it was almost threadbare and color-bare because of the blazing tropical sun. As I piled up this mound of rags, I thought of Susanna--maybe she could still get a few weeks of wear out of them.

The next time she came to visit, I offered her this pitiful heap. She was delighted and thanked me profusely: "Masome Jita, Masome Jita!" *Thank you, thank you,* and off she went.

Surprisingly, the next day she returned. I was busy packing and trying to get a month's work squeezed into the few days that remained before our departure. She lingered, watching me while I worked; I didn't have time to sit and visit.

Finally she came to the point of her visit. "Please, Nyango, I would like some shuss (shoes)."

I thought to myself, *What in the world would she ever want with my shoes? She has never worn shoes; they would never fit; and besides she could never navigate in shoes with heels.*

She pleaded, "Please Ma, please Ma."

Suddenly the thought struck me, *How selfish of her to ask for shoes after I gave her that pile of "good" clothes yesterday!*

George was working hard in the next room, getting ready to hand over the mission records, and as he heard my conversation with Susanna, he called out in jest, "Don't give away all your good shoes because they have at least another four years of wear in them!"

That did it! All the shoes that were left went to Susanna. She put on the pair with the highest heels and showed me how well they fit-- with *inches* to spare! She tied the rest in a bundle and hopped down the path singing, her feet going like eggbeaters.

George called out, "I hope you gave her some money for a hospital stay in case she breaks her neck with those shoes."

Our tasks intensified. One day our headmistress came to have her school records checked, and we were busily engaged in that task when up the path came barefooted Susanna. She was all smiles as she came triumphantly up onto the porch with a "dash," a gift. I thanked her, but being under pressure to finish "my work," I tried to usher her off. Missions records were of *most* importance.

Susanna could not read or write, but she wasn't ignorant, so with a hurt in her voice she asked, "You no hopen um?" *Won't you open my present?*

At that, I gained my missionary composure. "Oh yes, OH YES, I almost forgot."

As I peeled away the banana leaves in which the gift was wrapped, I expected to find some over-ripe eggs or fruit. Instead, out fell a piece of Ghana cloth with gold threads running through it--a prize that every African woman wanted but could not afford!

In amazement I cried, "Susanna, you can't give this to me! Where did you get the money to buy this?" *You can't! You can't!* my heart repeated.

This little saint looked up at me with questioning eyes. "You like um? You like um? You member your Pekin, Susanna?" *I want you to remember your child Susanna.* I choked back the tears, but my empty words were translated into an embrace.

As I went back to "my mission books," our headmistress interrupted my thoughts: "Please Ma, today I've seen at work the Gospel that you've been teaching all these years. I know where Susanna got the money to buy that gift for you. Yesterday I saw her in the market selling your shoes and old clothes to get it. She loves you plenty."

As a precious ointment poured on Jesus' feet, this too was an ointment that will never be forgotten. It was poured out for my departure. Susanna gave all that she had and kept nothing for herself, to show that she loved me--and I had misinterpreted that love--as millions still do today. I went to Africa to teach others, but I was taught by those whom Jesus touched, even those who could not read or write. I had learned the theological meaning of the word "love" at Toccoa Falls College, but it was in the jungles of Africa, taught by one who had never read the Word for herself, that I learned what Jesus really meant when He said: "By this shall all men know that ye are my disciples if you love one another as I have loved you" (John 13:15; 15:12).

Burkina Faso

A "CALLING CARD" IN BOBO-DIOULASSO

MICHELLE TATUM STANFORD

Michelle Tatum graduated from TFC in 1978. From there she went to Burkina Faso for six years. Since her marriage she has served with her husband in Britain.

As a nurse in the Bible school at Bobo-Dioulasso, I was also involved in evangelism and discipleship with the the women of the city, an exciting ministry.

One afternoon I had gone to a neighborhood called "Avion-so" (meaning "house of the plane," as the airport was within walking distance of that area). I had gone to spend the afternoon with a ladies' group. One of the members, "Nima," was a wonderful evangelist, full of boldness and creativity; I learned much as I followed her around that day.

First we had to decide how we would divide our group as we went out into the neighborhood to evangelize. At first the ladies suggested we go by two's, then by four's, or perhaps by five's. Finally it was suggested that we all minister together.

"We have a special 'calling card,'" one contributed. "Our missionary with her white skin will get us into many courtyards."

It was true. I was such an unusual-looking person (very few people had seen white people in that area) that indeed I could get us into almost any courtyard simply because of the color of my skin. Courtyard after courtyard opened the doors to us as the residents saw me--this unusual stranger curiously walking with the group.

As we sat with the extended family in each place, the ladies were able to share the gospel message with each family unit. What a wonderful afternoon!

My most vivid memory is that of an elderly lady we met on the pathway. We shared the Good News with her, and her eyes shone with excitement as she chose to make Jesus her Lord. She almost immediately took on an inner loveliness that shone through her face.

I reached to shake and hold her hand and was shocked to find that her fingers were now only nubs. Her ears were disfigured, as were her nose and her feet. Suddenly I realized that her life had been ravaged by leprosy, but she literally shone with radiance as she chose to "walk the Jesus Road."

Because I had been a "calling card," one day she would have a new and whole body in Heaven. Praise His name!

Côte d'Ivoire

ON THE LAST DAY!

JEAN HOTALEN

Jean and her husband Norwood Hotalen were houseparents for three years at Toccoa Falls following their marriage. Sensing the call to Africa, they spent three and a half terms as house parents for missionary children in Zaire. Since 1974 they have been house parents to MKs in Côte d'Ivoire under the auspices of the C&MA.

Marcelle (her name is really Zu-Hui Wang, but she took the name Marcelle while at our English-speaking school) was a giggly high school sophomore, more interested in how to get a boy to pay attention to her than in learning the spiritual truths I was trying to share with her. She was a bubbly, average-sized teenager with a perpetual grin on her face; we soon discovered that she had really come to the MK school in Côte d'Ivoire to perfect her English.

Her parents had come from Taiwan some years before, seeking to earn a better living working in agriculture here than might have been possible in their own country. Though they were Buddhists in name, they were not opposed to their daughter's attending a Christian school and hearing the gospel.

Marcelle was in my care group of four students. (Each staff member seeks to give special attention and care to four or five students so that every student knows there is at least one person vitally interested in him or her.) Marcelle would come to a "tea party" just for her and me whenever I invited her, and we'd talk easily about her--her studies, life in the dorm, boys, or whatever she wanted to discuss. Always we ended by reading some Bible verses together and examining their meaning. As Marcelle was unsaved, I yearned to introduce her to Jesus Christ who would transform her life. However, she seemed unable to grasp spiritual truths.

The year hurried along, and our furlough was nearing. Not knowing if I'd ever see Marcelle again, I was burdened to see her born again before the end of the school year. I earnestly asked God the Holy Spirit to work in her heart--but nothing was happening, at least that I could discern.

It was the last day of school. I was, to say the least, a harried dorm mother, with girls bombarding me with such questions as: "Aunt Jean, will you come check me out?" "Aunt Jean, I can't find my jeans I put in the wash." "Did you sign me up for a travel lunch?" Happy chaos was reigning in our dorm as girls were packing, and I was late getting to the dining hall to help make lunches for the students who were then leaving.

Just as I was ready to walk out the front door, who should come in but Marcelle! "Hello, Aunt Jean," she said in her soft, smiling voice. "Are you busy? Can we talk?"

Am I busy? Understatement of the year! I thought, but didn't say. "Good morning, Marcelle. Surely we can talk," I agreed in my sweetest voice, thinking all the while, *Now Father, this has to be short because I am very, very busy.*

I led her to a private sitting room, while many of my girls were left with their questions unanswered or demands unmet. I promised I'd be back as soon as possible.

Hoping her visit wouldn't take long, I asked Marcelle to sit down. We both sat on the couch, and she simply stated, "Aunt Jean, I want to become a Christian. Can you help me?"

I gasped, "YOU DO?" I was hardly able to believe

my ears. *Oh, Lord,* I thought, *You are too funny! Here it is the last day of the term when all chaos is breaking loose out there in the dorm, and this is the day and the time You choose to bring Marcelle into Your family!! Well, so be it. This is what it's all about. This takes priority over all.*

I went over the basics again, and Marcelle assured me she understood what I was saying. We knelt, and I told her she could ask Jesus into her heart in Chinese, as He understood Chinese perfectly. While she was praying, I heard Marcelle say something like "Jin wo de shin," and a light turned on in my head. When she finished, I prayed for her--then began singing:

"Jin wo de shin,
Jin wo de shin,
Lai jin wo de shin dru Yesu;
Shan zai jin lai,
Yong boo le kai,
Lai jin wo de shin dru Yesu."

As I was singing, kneeling beside her, her eyes lit up in recognition. When I finished, I asked, "Does that mean anything to you? Do you understand those words?"

She excitedly replied, "Yes, I understand! How do you know that song?" (I had sung the chorus, "Into my heart, into my heart, come into my heart, Lord Jesus" in Chinese.)

With some quick mental calculations, I answered, "Marcelle, I learned that song thirty-eight years ago when I was at a Bible conference. A missionary to China, Dr. Hamilton, taught it to me. I just remembered it when I heard you pray. I thought I heard 'Jin wo de shin,' and God Himself brought that little song back to my remembrance after all these years!"

We laughed and hugged and had some tears of joy

at the awesomeness of the moment. I was overwhelmed that God in His foreknowledge had had me learn that little chorus so long ago in Florida, so that when the day came that an American missionary lady would pray with a Chinese girl to receive Jesus into her heart in Africa, she could hear something about Him in her own language! What a loving Father He is!

At that, Marcelle was up and out the door. To some girls who were still waiting for me in the lounge, she called happily, "Do you know what? I just asked Jesus into my heart, and now I'm a Christian!" Joyous exclamations burst from the girls as they surrounded her, hugging and laughing. Soon she was running to her dorm to share her good news with her other friends.

As I went to make the sack lunches, I thought of how God had spoken so clearly to my heart through Dr. Hamilton at that youth conference at Mt. Dora and had put on my heart the burden to go as a missionary to continue the sharing of the gospel. He had led me to Toccoa Falls, prepared me for missionary service, and sent me to Africa with my husband.

Jin we de shin, Jin we de shin,

Is it coincidence that, while on furlough the year following Marcelle's conversion, we "ran into" Dr.

Hamilton in Atlanta, thirty-nine years since our first meeting? I was able to share with him how God had used the little chorus he had taught me in Chinese so many years before to help confirm a young girl's transaction with the Savior thirty-eight years later.

"Come in today,
Come in to stay,
Come into my heart, Lord Jesus!"

Côte d'Ivoire

WILLIAM, MOUSSA, AND RON

DONALD O. YOUNG

Dr. Donald O. Young and his wife were 1968 graduates of Toccoa Falls College. Former missionaries to Côte d'Ivoire, Dr. Young was recently Director of Missionary Candidates for the C&MA.

William

During the days of Power Encounter Evangelism from 1975-1979 in the Ivory Coast (Côte d'Ivoire), many exciting things happened in our ministry. One particular day we were working at the Bouake Youth Center where many thousands of high school students passed each day. We were the only evangelical voice to the several hundred thousand teens in the large city of Bouake, and we enjoyed a tremendous ministry. One afternoon one of my teen leaders, named Andre, brought in a friend whom he introduced as William. Andre proceeded to tell me the following thrilling story about the conversion of his friend.

William came from a pagan family, very well-known in his village. He had completed junior and senior high school with great ease. The village people were very proud of William and praised his family for honoring the fetish gods.

William was now in college. It was examination time; he was given money to see the village witch-doctor, who gave him a special potion made from the innards of a dead chicken and goat. He then was led to a small dark room with no windows and only one door. He was to spend the night in this dark room, rubbing his body with the terrible-smelling potion eighteen times over the next twenty-four hours. This he did, and each time he scrubbed his body with this potion, he thought he was putting extra intelligence into his mind for the coming examinations.

William returned to the capital city the next day for the examinations, certain that the fetish powers given him by the village magic man would help him pass. Imagine his despondency when the results were posted and he had failed. He could not believe his eyes . . . someone must have made a mistake . . . the power of the fetish was too strong.

William could not face the village people or his family. He wanted to die. He decided to go to the largest building in Abidjan and jump off. Maybe by dying in this manner he could redeem himself in people's eyes.

As he was climbing the steps to this large building, he met Andre, who was here celebrating his passing the tests. Andre could see that William looked discouraged.

"What's the matter, William?"

"I've failed the exam; I can't face my people; I'm on my way to the top of the building to jump off."

"Oh, no," cried Andre. "Don't! I have wonderful news for you," and as he talked to William that afternoon, he led him to the Lord.

William is now a pastor in one of the African churches. What a testimony of God's grace!

Moussa

The summer of 1967 I met a young boy named Moussa, whose story is almost unbelievable. From a Muslim family, he left his village some 200 miles away to attend school in Bouake, even though he had no place to live. He slept on the benches at school or under trees in the park. Someone told him about our Youth Center Dorm for Teens, and he came to see if there was any room. Unfortunately, there wasn't, but the Christian kids took care of him, and he eventually became a Christian.

When he returned to his village to tell his parents that he was a Christian, the family became very angry. His father demanded, "How could you? You know I'm a devout Muslim. You bring shame upon our house!"

His family did everything they could to persuade Moussa to renounce his new-found faith and return to his Muslim roots, but Moussa would not let family pressures change his mind.

"If you don't renounce your faith in this Christian God," his father finally shouted, "you are no son of mine. I'll take away your heritage and give it to another. You will be considered dead!" Angrily he stomped away.

Moussa would not renounce his faith. Soon the entire Muslim population gathered in the village for a funeral. Moussa attended *his own funeral!* After his "death" Moussa was banned from the village, to return to Bouake with no money and only the clothes on his back.

The Christians in Bouake gathered money and clothes for him, and Moussa was cared for through his school years until he graduated and became a pastor. Although only thirteen years old when he was converted, Moussa has since returned to his village as a pastor, and many of his family have become Christians.

Ron

Our son Ron, home from MK school for a short visit, was bitten on the lips by our puppy. Ron didn't tell any of us because he felt the puppy was just playing. At the end of the week Ron returned to Ivory Coast Academy.

A few days later, the puppy suddenly died. Then our houseboy told us that, while we were away, a mad dog had come into our yard and bitten our puppy. The houseboy hadn't realized how serious this matter was. We took the puppy to the local veterinarian who had tests made and shocked us by telling us that our puppy had died of rabies. He told us to find, as soon as possible, all of the people who had been touched by the puppy. Everyone in our family needed to get a series of seven rabies shots.

When I asked Ron by phone, he told us of the puppy's biting him on the lips. Frightened, we rushed to the doctor with this knowledge. I shall never forget his words: "I'm sorry . . . there is nothing we can do for your son. The rabies shots won't help. He has been bitten on the face, and the poison will go straight to the brain. It will only be a matter of time."

We were crushed . . . our oldest son Ron . . . can die a horrible death from rabies. The word spread.

Thousands of people worldwide went to prayer for Ron. People we never knew, years later told us of their prayers for him.

Because the symptoms were beginning to appear . . . pain in the joints . . . high fever . . . dreams, Ron was asked to leave the MK school. One night Marlen and I were crying to God. Finally, we prayed, "Lord, You gave Ron to us. We gave him back to You. Therefore, he is in Your hands!"

I cannot explain the peace that came over us, but God met us as we prayed; we knew Ron would be all right.

Within days the fever left; the pains were gone. Again we went to see the doctor. He took a blood sample and had it sent to the U.S. Center for Disease Control in Atlanta. Word came back in one week's time: "No sign of any rabies' material in the blood; the boy is cleared."

Praise God for His constant care over us during those days in Africa.

Gabon

MIRACLE IN AN AFRICAN NIGHT

ANITA READER

After nurses' training, Toccoa Falls College, and a summer tour in Ecuador in AYC, Anita Reader responded to the call to Africa. There she has worked in a dispensary and taught children's Bible classes. She is now working in medical and district ministries in Bongolo.

One of my greatest fears and trials during my first term in Gabon was learning to drive a 4-wheel drive vehicle. Having lived in Florida most of my life, I was used to driving a small car on flat, straight, paved roads. In Gabon I had to drive a 4-wheel double-clutching vehicle over mountainous, muddy, slippery roads--a very large undertaking for a Florida girl!

During my first four years I had several major breakdowns, but was always close to help. On one particular occasion I realized that I was having a problem with the truck and decided to go to Bongolo to get help, as there were no service stations near where I was living. A mechanic in Bongolo checked out the problem and worked on it. Assured that the truck was repaired, I left Bongolo about 4 P.M. with a truck full of people who wanted to get back to our village twenty-five miles away.

Suddenly, about fifteen miles out of Bongolo, I realized that I was having the same problem as before: the brakes were jamming. One of the back wheels was not turning; therefore, the tire was burning rubber.

I was fifteen miles from help. No gas stations, no telephones, and usually no traffic on this road after dark. There *was* a ferry not far away, but it did not operate after 6 P.M. unless there was an emergency.

Someone suggested, "Let's all go to the next village." I felt I had to stay with the truck. Finally, everyone decided to stay with me.

We had no food. What to do? One of the men volunteered to walk the ten miles to our village to let everyone know what had happened to us.

At this point I realized: *I don't need just another truck to come by, but I need someone with some knowledge about mechanics!* Such persons in Gabon are very few. We waited and prayed, not knowing what was going to happen--but God did.

An hour passed. Darkness came.

Suddenly, we tensed. What did we hear? Could it be? Yes, it was the motor of a vehicle. What excitement! Could help be coming?

Soon a truck stopped. Two men hopped out. As I stammered my problem, one of the men assured me: "Maybe I can help; I'm a mechanic from a town nearby."

After getting his tools, he soon repaired my truck; now I could continue the trip to my station. All piled back into the truck, happy that they'd get home. The mechanic even followed us to be sure we'd arrive safely.

That's not luck: that's God!

You cannot understand the significance of this happening unless you can understand how very slim the chances were for a truck to pass by at that time of night, *and* for the person in that truck to be a mechanic.

THE TRUCK TWICE-OWNED

What happened to my new blue truck? Had it been stolen? Who had taken it?

These were some of the questions that flashed through my mind when I realized that my truck was missing.

After I had received permission from our headquarters to purchase a truck, I had immediately written to the churches in the States concerning the need. Soon the Lord had provided me with a beautiful blue Toyota truck to be used in my various ministries. Now it was gone!

It happened one Friday afternoon in January. I had gone to Bongolo for a few days. Because I had been unable to use the ferry to transport the truck to the other side of the river, I had locked it and left it on the Lebamba side and crossed over in a canoe. Other missionaries had often parked their vehicles there.

"Your truck is missing!" Rudely my quiet Sunday afternoon was interrupted with these frightening words.

"I'll check," one of the missionaries promised, but he did not return soon.

"It must be true; my truck's been stolen. I must report it at once to the police."

Prayers of my coworkers and national brethren greatly encouraged me; however, humanly thinking, we all realized that the recovery of the truck was unrealistic.

After the field chairman had been informed of the theft, he checked with the police in Mouila to be sure they had been notified.

"We have," they assured him, "and not only that, but we've received news that a Toyota has been stopped two miles from the Congo border." Surely it was mine! Praise God!

The next day we drove to Malinga to verify that the truck was really mine. It had suffered minor damage, but otherwise was in good condition.

This incident increased not only my faith but also the faith of the nationals. Once again God had revealed to all of us the power of prayer. The unbelievers could contribute the recovery of the truck to no one else but God. Only God could have stopped the truck a mere two miles from the border.

We read in the Bible, "with God all things are possible." I thank God for this portion of scripture and what it means to me.

A blue truck twice-owned was definitely an answer to prayer.

"Trust in the Lord with all thine heart; and lean not unto thine own understanding. In all thy ways acknowledge Him and He shall direct thy paths" (Proverbs 3:5-6).

These verses have given me strength and hope many, many times in my missionary career. God has shown me His faithfulness in situations when I could do nothing for myself. The two accounts above demonstrate His care and provision for me.

Gabon

BLESSINGS IMMEASURABLE

CLARENCE WALKER

Clarence and Phyllis (Brewster) Walker went to Gabon in 1962, where they labored faithfully. After Phyllis' death in 1979 in the States, he went back to Gabon, where the Lord gave him a new helpmate. They are serving the Lord in Libreville.

What an exciting time to be in the little country of Gabon, Africa! Next year I shall complete my sixth term here, and never before has there been such tremendous growth in the church. The main congregation in the capital city of Libreville, where we are in church planting ministry, has a total attendance of 3,000 Africans who worship in one of two services each Sunday morning. There are four smaller Alliance churches. The city has a total population of 350,000. We have the privilege of witnessing a harvest that is the result of many years of planting, watering, and nurturing by former missionaries and national workers. And to think-- but for a vital decision made twelve years ago, I could have missed this wonderful blessing, as well as many others!

In 1976, Phyllis and I, along with our three children, left Gabon for our third furlough in the States. We had served in village ministries, in the Bible school, and for two years as chairman of the field.

After our furlough year and a two-year leave of absence, we were anticipating our return in 1979 to Gabon. A 4x4 Toyota was purchased, barrels were being packed, and there was general excitement. Then in November, Phyllis came down with an undiagnosed illness, later identified as cancer.

Though friends and loved ones around the world prayed, she became progressively worse, and on February 17, 1979, the Lord saw fit to take her home to Glory. Phyllis' peace in the midst of suffering and pain was an inspiration to all of us.

The weeks that followed were not easy, but God's grace comforted and sustained us. In time a decision was imperative concerning my return to the field. Deborah, my older daughter, was in her third year of pre-med at Hope College. Lauralyn (12) and Stan (10) were eager to return to Africa, which they considered "home." Many well-meaning friends and relatives counseled me against going, saying it would be an irresponsible move for a single father. There was no leading from the Lord that I could detect, however, except to go ahead with plans to return to Gabon as scheduled. In July Lauralyn, Stan, and I arrived in Libreville.

Our assignment, communicated to us before Phyllis' illness, was to minister in the business office and guest house in Libreville. Now it was decided that I would care for the business office and that the Roland Bowmans, involved in church planting there, would temporarily take care of the guest house. The arrangement worked well. Lauralyn and Stan went to our missionary children's school at Bongolo in September.

That first year was not easy emotionally, but I enjoyed the work the Lord had given me, and He continued to give the same grace He had so wonderfully supplied during our last months in the States.

The relatively new Alliance work in the capital city had already begun to grow. Until very recently the C&MA missionaries in Gabon had concentrated their efforts in the southern half of the country. However, with the migration of Alliance Christians from the south to Libreville and other northern cities, the call eventually came for someone to "come over and help us." Beginning with a few believers, the church was steadily growing and by 1979 ready to build its first permanent sanctuary. Though I was not directly involved in church planting at that time, it was good to be in Libreville and to be a part of the work.

Since I traveled a great deal as business agent, I was able to visit the children several times. That, along with their vacation times with me, was a great morale booster. Nothing, however, could remove the loneliness and void that we all felt without Phyllis. The things she had done for us and all that she was to us, much of which had been taken for granted, were sorely missed. The kids were great! After three years away from Africa, they were glad to be back. Though hurting, they adjusted well socially and were sustained spiritually. Relatives in the States rallied around Deborah, who continued to do well in her studies.

Inevitably, as there were many single ladies on our field and since my married colleagues were eager to play the role of Cupid, the possibility that perhaps the Lord had another partner in mind for me (and a stepmother for my children) loomed large before me. It seemed incredible that after all those months of thinking that such a relationship would be impossible in the wake of a wonderful first marriage, the Lord was beginning to make me realize that not only could it be possible, but that in His will it could be the best thing for us. But how was I to know? What would be the sign? I was determined that I, with the Lord--and *not* my well-meaning colleagues--would make the decision!

The signs that followed were many; the Lord's choice was Marcia Dunn, a first-term missionary nurse. It was amazing how quickly the Lord confirmed to both Marcia and me that it was indeed He who was bringing us together. There was an almost immediate bond between Marcia and the children, including Deborah when they later met one another.

After a beautiful wedding on the field and a brief honeymoon, we assumed our duties as a team in the guest house and business office in Libreville for the remainder of the term.

The following term I was field director. Since 1988 we have been in church planting ministry in Libreville, and Marcia has been director of Christian literature sales for the field. I was again assigned to the office of field director in June of 1991.

Deborah studied medicine in Michigan State University and became a medical doctor. She is now a pediatrician at our mission hospital here in Gabon. Lauralyn and Stan and their spouses, after studying at TFC, are accredited candidates for missionary work with the C&MA. The Lord has blessed Marcia and me with two additional daughters, Cynthia (10) and Stephanie (8). They are attending the MK school at Bongolo and have endeared themselves to the entire family.

The decision that the Lord helped me make in 1979--to return to Gabon--ushered my family and me into a decade of immeasurable blessing that I am certainly glad we didn't miss! As a fellow Toccoa Falls quartet member of mine, David Eckman, used to sing back in the 1950's, "God leads His dear children along!"

Mali

BE READY TO PREACH, PRAY, OR DIE

DOLORIS BURNS BANDY

Doloris and Tom Burns were C&MA missionaries in Mali for thirty-nine years. After Tom's tragic death, Doloris became the wife of Dr. Julian A. Bandy, now chancellor of Toccoa Falls College.

As students at Toccoa Falls College, a small interdenominational college in north Georgia, we often heard, "Be prepared to preach, pray, or die on a moment's notice." In fact, it became an unofficial motto when ministry assignments were often given at the last minute. These short notices were sometimes met with a grumbling response.

That slogan, however, "Be prepared to preach, pray, or die on a moment's notice," became the operating principle of the life of my husband, Tom Burns. God had called him as a young man to preach, and it seemed he was always prepared whether in English, French, or Dogon (a tribal language in northern Mali). We served there for thirty-nine years.

Often on our way to a service, or perhaps at the last red light, he would turn and say, "By the way, Doloris, would you mind giving a word of testimony tonight?" And if my response held negative "vibes," he verbally wondered why I wasn't always as prepared as he. Whether for a church service or a funeral, he practiced this principle. I've seen him on several occasions get up in the middle of the night to officiate at a funeral, still pajama-clad. In the intense heat of sub-Sahara climate, a person is buried immediately without embalming. There is no time to prepare.

A woman with her three-year-old son in tow came one morning to our clinic in Sangha. The charms around her neck, her arms, and her waist told me that she was a heathen who knew only the fear of evil spirits and nothing of the love of God. Receiving treatment for parasites week after week, she heard God's plan for salvation for her life. The message began to penetrate her heart and she accepted Christ as Savior. As she lived in the medical guest room for so long, we learned to know Yana well. We learned that not only was she bound by evil spirits, but that she had had fifteen husbands. "What would one do with fifteen husbands?" you might ask. The reason, however, that she had acquired so many men was that she was childless. In Africa for a woman to be without children is a "shame matter." This stigma impelled her to "marry" man after man until finally she bore a child, a son.

One morning before dawn, Asegerema, the white-bearded translator, knocked on our door to inform us that Yana had died in her sleep with the little boy still nursing at her side. He added with a twinkle, "And you, Mr. Burns, will preach the funeral as soon as the body is prepared for burial." This would be in approximately an hour.

This time Tom was not prepared to preach! *What could one say about a new convert who had had fifteen husbands?* As Tom prayed for wisdom, God directed his reading to Hebrews, chapter eleven, God's hall of fame. There he read of the faith of Abraham, the faith of David, the faith of Moses, and of many others who exercised great faith. There was nothing, however, concerning Abraham's unbelief, David's adultery, Moses' anger, or Rahab's prostitution. God remembered their sins no more! Tom breathed, "Thank you, Lord," and preached the funeral. He was prepared!

One time, just returning from furlough and before our baggage arrived, we made a trip to the sandy plains of the district in the sub-Sahara region south of Timbuktu, among the Dogon people. We took only our sleeping mats with us to unfold in the back of the truck at night and coffee to add to the breakfast menu of cooked millet mush. This was primarily a trip to visit the pastors and fellow Christians, not an evangelistic or teaching effort.

Greetings play an important role in African culture. One never embarks on any conversation without first engaging in the formalities of lengthy greetings. Thus, when we pulled into the church yard at Dominusogu and the pastor came to the car and simply asked without first greeting, "Do you have any medicine with you?" we were surprised.

My husband quickly answered, "No, Ogupema, we have only just returned from our 'father's country' and came only to give greetings. We did not bring the medicine box." He continued, "We can, however, send a cyclist to our French school to get what you need. . . . "

Immediately the Holy Spirit's inner prompting spoke to him, saying, "Tom, I am here. Trust Me."

Getting out of the car, Tom turned to the pastor, Pema, apologizing, "We don't need a cyclist; call the Christians together."

As our eyes became accustomed to the darkness in the little mud brick church, I saw Rute, the wife of another pastor, sitting on a grass mat. In her lap was the lifeless form of a tiny baby. This limp form had not nursed for three days.

Pema blew the old cow horn, summoning the village Christians to the church. When they hear the sound of that horn, the Christians drop whatever they are doing and gather immediately into the tiny mud brick chapel. They too saw Rute bent over her lifeless baby. As we knelt on the grass mats encircling Rute, the elders and pastors anointed and prayed for baby Rebeka. Before they had finished praying, the power of God surged through this lifeless child, and she reached up, took her mother's breast, and nursed!

We are told: "Pray without ceasing." This means that we're to be ready to exercise our faith in prayer at a moment's notice. We did not have time to "go into our closet" and catch up on our prayers. It was necessary to exercise that faith in prayer at a moment's notice!

And as Tom lived, prepared to preach, prepared to pray, so he died--with a prepared heart.

He was building our "dream house" for retiral on property close to Toccoa Falls campus--and he loved it. He had built so many houses in Africa, but this one was special, and he was excited about it. Every spare hour after work was given to planning, purchasing, and working.

One Saturday morning in November, he left the house at 6 o'clock to work with the builder. He kissed me goodbye and said, "Doloris, I'm going up to the house. I put a note on the refrigerator door for you." He knew that at 6 o'clock in the morning, he could not give me any instructions. They would not have registered. Later, when I did get up, I found his note with instructions concerning the errands he wanted me to do that day. My daughter Nansie Ike was visiting.

We had just returned home from our last errand of the day when the builder, Jim McCollum, appeared at the door and stated, "Doloris, Tom has fallen." He continued, "He is in the emergency room at the hospital; I think you should come." He went on to assure me that Tom would be all right, not to worry.

We quickly found a baby sitter and Nansie and I went to the hospital. *But* he wasn't all right. He was transferred to Athens, Georgia, for neurosurgery. Tom remained comatose for five days, never regaining consciousness. When he fell from the first floor onto the cement basement floor, he had no advance notice, no warning. No time to prepare. But as Tom lived, so he died--with a prepared heart!

The often-repeated slogan when we were in college--be prepared to preach, to pray, or to die on a moment's notice--is still a guiding principle of my life as it was of my husband, Tom. We need always to be ready to give an answer for the HOPE that is in us--to share our faith. We need always to be ready to exercise our faith in prayer with a friend. We need always to keep our heart in readiness to meet our Savior!

Nigeria

CONTRASTS: LIGHT AND DARKNESS

GOLDIE BLAKENEY

Goldie Blakeney, from Nova Scotia, is a three-time graduate of Toccoa Falls: from high school in 1940 and from college in 1948; then in 1987, she received the honorary degree of Doctor of Letters (Lit.D.). She served under the Sudan Interior Mission in Nigeria from 1948 to 1990.

The prospects of life can change quickly in missionary service: like clouds scudding through a darkening sky, sometimes obscuring the sun, but ultimately yielding to its powerful rays. Such was my experience as a missionary teacher in Nigeria.

Midway through my career, appointment came to teach the Bible in state-run high schools. Could teaching the Bible with non-Christian and nominal Christian national staff members in a government-approved curriculum be called missionary work? And then to open a Department of Religious Studies in a Federal College of Education? Would my prayer partners at home continue to pray for such a ministry? The Mission approved, saying I should take a leave of absence, if necessary, to buy up the opportunity to train national teachers in this discipline.

Clouds appeared. Several times thieves broke into my little mission home. A young domestic worker found a four-inch black scorpion on my doorstep! Another day I returned from a Sunday morning student service and drove through a frenzied crowd of traditional African religionists on the road, only to lie down at home for my needed siesta to see a viper hanging from the ceiling of my bedroom. But I *did* see it, and good missionary neighbors came and rescued me from "dangers seen."

Darker clouds also appeared as ungodly, nominal Christian teachers sought to take over the lectures and manage the department in such a way that the true Light of the Word would be obscured. His radiance broke through, nevertheless. What a joy to be joined to the Son Himself in the exciting ministry of sharing His Way and Truth and Life with Nigerian youth!

Imagine what it was like to teach the Gospel of John to forty college students. How far could you go, even in an academic setting, without presenting Jesus as the true Light? These same students required my attention in approving their work plans for teaching Bible Knowledge in twenty schools of three states for six weeks' teaching practice. My help was needed in preparing visual aids for the Bible lessons, followed by supervision of their work in those secondary schools, and in each place leaving behind a witness for Christ.

Opportunities abounded to sponsor the Christian Students' Fellowship Group on campus, though clouds again threatened to blot out the light. The Palm Wine Drunkards, a student club, delighted in drumming, chanting, dancing, and imbibing in a nearby palm grove. When one of their number was witnessed to and saved, he literally forsook the powers of darkness for the Light of Life in Jesus.

Can you see me leaving the week-day activities at the college and fulfilling the role of a "real" missionary? Like going to an isolated community on Sunday morning to encourage a handful of believers meeting in a temporary shelter because a tropical storm had blown the roof off their little church building. Then being asked to visit a blind *mama* sitting at home on a grass mat in the literal darkness of a mud-walled room. There I shared the Good

News of salvation through faith in the Lord Jesus Christ. She had heard it before, but that morning she opened her heart to receive the Light of the World. With glowing face she sang, to a familiar native tune, words of trust in Jesus.

Or follow me to sponsor an evening Fellowship of Christian Students at a nearby secondary school, where 125 teenaged boys have invited me to speak on "Jesus the Bread of Life." Afterwards, an eleventh grader comes up to me with a seventh grader in tow.

"Please, this boy joined us last week at the rally. He was a Muslim before, but he has now decided to follow Jesus!"

Oh, for more Andrews! For me, it is the joy of discipleship as I see the older boy, himself scarcely more than a lad, bringing his bright-eyed little "brother" to Jesus.

Then there was that special week of victory at the college. The Christian Fellowship Group invited a powerful Nigerian evangelist to come for a series of week-night meetings. Much prayer and effort went into the arrangements for each meeting on the federal government campus. Students from many academic disciplines, made up of a variety of ethnic groups from several states in the Federation, attended. The college is situated near a thickly populated town of 100,000 people who are largely Muslim and traditional religionists, with only a few small pockets of Christians in the area.

Each evening sweet songs of praise and salvation arose to the Lord, often accompanied by rhythmic clapping and converted drums and guitars. We prayed. We heard the Word of God read. Gospel light beamed into darkened hearts! By the end of that campaign, eighty had made decisions for Christ. All eighty were Nigerian men and women in a college of education, training to be teachers of various subjects at the secondary level. We were excited about the potential for future Christian leadership and the divine multiplication that could evolve from such an event. Fifty of the eighty turned up for a "follow-up" discipleship class that I, as the only missionary teacher among the leaders, taught for six weeks.

Coincident with the presence of Christ in His people came thunderheads of the "powers of darkness." Men having a "form of godliness but denying the power thereof" wanted to run their own Department of Religious Studies at the college. They had the qualifications on paper; I was the "outsider." They needed the work; I was a volunteer. I withdrew from the classroom lectures, but continued the discipleship classes and other Christian activities on campus.

One dark night, at about 10 o'clock, I was nearing the end of the lonely ten-mile trip home from the college. Exhausted, but rejoicing in a particular victory which had been won for Christ that night, I turned into the last stretch of narrow dirt road leading to the mission compound. To my horror, the headlights of my VW revealed a tight mass of many hundreds of men and boys in the road separating me from home. Their sacred "juju" celebration was taking place, and I had not been informed. All women were safely hidden behind the mud walls of their homes: for them it was strictly forbidden to see what was being done.

The milling masses of celebrants closed in behind me. I was surrounded by drunken, drumming, dancing, devil-inspired men.

Someone asked if I were a man! Others demanded payment of a goat for violating their sacred taboo! Still others shouted obscure threats.

Surrounded by a thick cloud of spiritual darkness such as this, I was too stunned to pray consciously. But there was a sweet consciousness that someone, somewhere, was praying for this missionary.

As the men beat upon my poor little VW with their sticks, I remembered having seen from the safe distance of my mission home their nonstop orgies lasting sometimes for forty-eight hours. I was painfully aware that they could not maintain this pitch without the help of witchcraft connected with their pagan juju. I quickly locked both doors and rolled up the windows of the car.

Suddenly, out of the mass of men appeared one with a familiar, friendly face! As a believer he ought not to have been there, but I believe God sent him as a ray of light to help overcome the darkness that night: a guardian angel in human form!

"You absolutely cannot pass through the men between here and the mission," he yelled. "You must go back."

He got into the car to help me. I knew it was well-nigh impossible to reverse, but the Lord gave me *super-Goldie* ability as my protector kept shouting at the mob to let me "reverse back" (as they say) to the junction. Great clusters of men gave way for us as he guided me to a hidden narrow trail which led to the mission compound from another direction.

My coworker was amazed to see me. Only after I had left, had she learned what was to take place that night, and she had not expected to see me until the next day. Weary and trembling, but triumphant, we had a little praise meeting and went peacefully to our rest.

Dark clouds still scud across the Nigerian sky attempting to blot out God's light. A recent editorial (1990) in a North American paper referred to the very area in which the above incident occurred. In the town where I lived, ritual murder is on the increase; in another local area, dealers have been selling human skulls for $5000.00; just across the neighboring border, human fetuses are on sale in the marketplace for the practice of magic rituals.

On the religio-political side, churches are being destroyed; Christians are being denied positions of leadership; discrimination is being felt against Christian student activities in public schools.

Yet the Light of the Gospel of our Lord Jesus Christ shone in the hearts of my students of yesterday who have become today's leaders in many homes, schools, churches, and communities, and He radiates through their lives as a visible witness. The darkness shall never overcome it. Praise!

Sudan

SOWING FOR CHRIST IN DINKALAND

TRAVIS MCDONALD

Travis and Evelyn McDonald began serving the Lord in Sudan in early 1950, as representatives of the Sudan Interior Mission. After twelve years there, they went to Ethiopia for two years. In 1989-1990 they served in Bolivia.

Behold, a sower went forth to sow. . . . Let us just suppose that that sower is your representative for Christ in Dinkaland.

And when he sowed, some seeds fell by the wayside, and the fowls came and devoured them. This is the sower's heartache, to see the precious seed devoured without having first brought forth its life. Typical of this seed is Deng, the witchdoctor, whom we have met with twice and on each occasion have had opportunity to sow the precious seed. Deng is the very picture of one given over to Satan. All the ornaments of sorcery, black magic, and every evil practice are on his body. The people sit in fear of him, yet they bring their sick ones to him to enslave further in darkness. He is supposed to have several evil spirits in his body, and no one would doubt that there are those who have died by his power.

Deng listened to the new Word with interest, but upon hearing that this Word could release from Satan's power, he closed his heart because "he loved darkness rather than the light." And again, we saw the fowls of this world devour the seed. How poignant with meaning to the Dinkas is the expression "sitting in darkness." The Dinkas have a legend which says that their forefathers came to their country during the dark nights when the moon was absent, and they say they are still in the "dark nights."

Some fell upon stony places, where they had not much earth; and forthwith they sprang up and when the sun was up, they scorched and withered. Panomdit (the village of the high head) is far away and had been seldom visited. When we were there Lual listened with real heart hunger and believed so far as he knew how. The Word meant release and a new way, and was received with gladness. But there was so little of the *earth* of teaching in the Word, and then too there was the hot sun of village ostracism and walking alone to fight. As is so often the case, the precious seedling scorched and withered. It is heart-rending to think of getting to a village only once a year, but we just weren't able to do more.

When we finally returned to Panomdit, we found Lual scorched and withering. Praise God for the reviving power of the water of God's Word. As he again heard the story and was again assured of its truth, hope revived, and we do believe he is still trusting the Lord.

And some fell among thorns, and the thorns sprang up and choked them. Satan has his thorn patches everywhere and seems to suit them to the surroundings. In Dinkaland it is often the love for the pagan dance, or the pleasure in being well-dressed with mud on the face and the body covered with bones, ashes, and skins. So much of the seed in Dinkaland is lost and covered up by the thorn patches.

Akel Padiet was a boy who finished our four years of elementary school and went away for secondary education. When we first came to Dinkaland, he was such a fine boy. He seemed really to love the things of God. He had been in school long enough to take on the polish and manners of civilization. All in all, he was most likable.

And then, somewhere along the way, the thorns of the world got a hold in his heart, and he began to lose out spiritually. The last time we saw him we hardly recognized him behind the wealth of Dinka mud, beads, bones, and bracelets. His wrists were broken open with ulcerous sores caused by the tight arm bracelets; every Dinka youth must be able to show scars from his bracelets. He was far more interested in his "glory" than he was in the Word of the Lord.

But other fell into good ground and brought forth fruit. Thank God for the hearts that were "good soil."

In early May in 1958 we had a special time of fellowship and Bible teaching at Banjang, seventy miles away from our station. Let me share a testimony that I will always remember.

Oliou, a Shilluk, spoke, but with great fear. It is not easy for a Shilluk to speak of things of the heart in another language. He exhorted the believers to go on with the Lord and not be turned back. Several times he exhorted, "Let us not tire!"

Then he turned to two large Bible pictures on the

wall behind him and asked, "Now which one of these means the most to us who love Jesus?"

One was a picture of the maimed, blind, and sick coming to Jesus for healing. The other one was the picture of the midnight hour at Calvary when the Son of God was forsaken on the cross.

Oliou continued, "Most people would choose this picture (pointing to the Healer), but to us who know Him as Savior, we choose this one and will follow Him (the picture of the Sin-Bearer)."

To me that was a simple way of getting across a great truth. The half-Christian world loves the Jesus who heals the blind, feeds the thousands, and stills the troubled sea, but His redeemed ones realize that apart from Calvary we have no sin-bearer. Thank God for the "Olioues"!

And then there was Aman. A believer of only eight months, he seemed to show promise of full payment for the long hours of personal teaching, counseling, and reprimands that were given him.

For awhile recently we feared we had failed, as we discovered that he had picked up a shotgun shell from our place and taken it home. Although others saw him with it, he strongly denied the act. We seemed up against an insurmountable blockage. His keenness was dulling noticeably. We continued to pray for him and teach him when possible. In Dinka ethics, nothing is wrong unless one is caught.

Soon I found him in another act of deceit, and we had *very strong talk*. The Word's condemnation for deceit and lying was read to him; finally, he broke down in real repentance. We felt so strongly that if he did not come clean over these matters he would be lost to real usefulness to the Lord. After that, he began to become more of a joy to teach. Then he attended a Christian conference at Chali and came home full of the joy of the Lord. In telling me about it, he kept slapping my arm in delight and exulting, "Chief, my heart was so satisfied, it almost tore open!"

Shortly after, he came asking to speak to me. I'd noticed that he seemed heavy-hearted. He shared his burden briefly: "Chief, my heart is very heavy. I awake in the morning with a weight on my heart, and I always know what it is. You remember my uncle who died in Abaiyath with kalazar. He was the closest male relative and left two wives, the younger one having been married on behalf of another dead brother. (All Dinka men who die unmarried must have a relative to marry a wife for him and rear children to his name; otherwise, great curses follow.)

"Now our clan has met and decided that I must take this younger wife. The talk began a month ago, and I refused strongly despite threats and pleas. They fear further deaths in the family if this wife does not bear children in behalf of the dead man.

"I have stated that I had rather leave home and lose all the family cows. I told them I was born again and could no longer walk in the ways of our people in such matters. My heart is continually troubled about this. My decision to refuse is firm, but it separates me from my family, and I'm asking the Lord to work so as to settle this without cutting me off from my people.

"I want my mother to believe. She says it is good the way I now walk, but the witch doctor is pestering her terribly. He has visited her several times reporting, 'Every time I throw the seven witchcraft stones (used to discern the fate of people), they read that some member of your family is going to die. They always read thus! You must let me have a sacrifice to lightning for you. Find three rams for the sacrifice and a cow and a calf to pay me. It is the spirit of lightning that threatens and must be appeased.'

"Because Jesus has taken away my confusion, I know that the evil spirit cannot bring death, and I see the cleverness of the witch doctor, but my mother is fearful."

Such situations are a real challenge and opportunity to teach these young babes in Christ to trust the Lord, to cast their burdens on Him, and to realize that he *hath not given us the spirit of fear; but of power, and love, and of a sound mind.* We beseech you to pray for these people.

Sudan

OUR HEATHEN SISTERS IN DINKALAND

EVELYN MCDONALD

While serving in the Sudan, Evelyn McDonald wrote about the situation of the women there. Through the years the conditions have changed little.

Heathendom seems to fall heaviest upon the women of Africa, leaving them completely downcast and without hope.

In Dinkaland we found the women far more difficult to reach than the men. The toll taken upon them by their heathen life has left them so destitute that they sometimes believe they have no souls. Physically and spiritually they are the slaves of man and Satan. The fact that they are married with cattle (cattle are given to purchase them as wives) only increases their servitude.

Their work is much heavier than the man's. See them trudging miles without shoes to bring huge pots of water! See them bending over the stones grinding calabash of grain for the beer-drinks, working under the burning sun. All their food is prepared by crushing the grain between a small stone as it is pushed over a larger one. See the Dinka woman, literally the mule of Dinkaland, taking the family possessions to the cattle camp upon her head. The basket on her head holds the baby, if she is fortunate to have one still alive. On top of the baby basket is piled the family sleeping skins, drinking gourds, grain, some stinking dried fish, and the two or three family chickens.

Even this would be bearable if she knew love and appreciation in her home, but these graces are unknown to the heathen vocabulary. Here is Akuot, one of three wives. She has no children and is continually sacrificing and pleading with Dengdit, the rain god, to remove the curse from her and give her children. Any woman without children is despised. Her much sacrificing and physical suffering at the hands of cruel witch doctors give her no children; her husband pushes her aside and marries another woman. When her husband dies, she will just be passed on to another member of the family, along with the sheep and cattle. The Dinka woman often has occasion to wail, "I'm only the slave. I have cattle upon my back, and I am not my own."

Our Dinka sister could bear up under the physical strain plus the lack of love, if only she knew the love of the Savior--if only she knew the Burden-Bearer who said, "Come unto Me and I will give you rest."

Alas, where this peace and love are so much needed, here reigns only heathen fear and darkness. With everything that touches her life, there is usually some superstition and fear connected. Birth, death, marriage, life, and work bear the dark imprint of heathendom. Even the greatest of natural loves, motherly love, has to give way to pagan fear.

Let me tell you of Gai. Some years ago she gave birth to a mentally abnormal child. Mother love was so strong that she refused to throw it into the river at birth. Despite the jeers, threats, and warnings, she kept the child near her side. Family, village, and all feared that keeping this child surely displeased the gods and would bring wrath upon them. For three years her strong mother love battled the fear in her heart as well as the protests around her. She was often seen drudging near the mission compound with her cumbersome load. No one would touch the child; the father in great fear was threatening to leave. Finally, with great heaviness of heart, she was seen walking alone. When asked where the baby was, she replied that it had died naturally. We knew better. Heathen fear had finally conquered mother love.

Still vivid is the picture of two old ladies sitting on the ground in the shade of a hut in Panomdit village. Returning from a session in the luak (cow barn), I stopped to speak to them. They were thrilled to have a little attention (the aged are rarely noticed). I quickly noticed that both were practically blind. I asked, "My mothers, what are you hoping in? You are very old. What is your hope?"

Practically together they replied, "We have nothing to hope in. We are aged and our spirits have died within us."

"But, mothers, you can have something to hope in. The Great Creator loves you and will give you life after death if you'll only hope in His Son."

At the mention of the Creator, their darkened minds could only conceive of Dengdit, and they replied with eyes heavenward and then in worship, kissing their hands, "Yes, we can hope in Dengdit, the son of Abuk. He sends the rain and will help us."

Twice I returned to these two old blind grandmothers and tried to penetrate their darkness with the wonderful story of God the Creator, showing Himself and His love through His only begotten Son. Only the Holy Spirit can penetrate the darkness, and we trust Him to do just that.

Are you burdened for these black women of Africa: the Akuots and the Gais? Their lot--only fear, superstition, and mule-work. We beseech you: pray for them!

And prayers *are* answered! It was such a joy to have about six women in a recent service--the highest number we'd ever had. Two recently professed the Lord at the Abaiyath clinic. Reaching the women has been difficult, and we often felt buffeted. These women almost disrupted the service with their enthusiastic comments on every song and word. Despite several reminders that the audience does not speak out so much in church, they continued to do so. They had been delivered from darkness to eternal light!

Yes, it pays to pray for these; there are so many still destitute, so many needing deliverance. Please pray!

ASIA

Arabian Sea

Pacific Ocean

years we covered most of the Bible. Through the Bible studies and prayer, God began to work in our midst as we prayed for their sons and other needy people who crossed our paths in the course of our daily work. It was during this time that Bhaskar shared with us his story.

"When I was ten or eleven, my family recognized that I had contracted leprosy. They turned me out of our home because of their fear of being ostracized by our neighbors. I was so frightened; I didn't know what to do or where to go. I had heard of a leprosy clinic in a city some distance away, so I went there. I was admitted, but before long I ran away and hopped on trains without a ticket, hoping I could find a place where I could be healed instantly. Finally, when I realized that I must be admitted for a period of time to receive treatment, I arrived at the Christian Leprosy Hospital near here. A kind Christian nurse admitted me and showed great kindness to me."

Bhaskar took the painful injections regularly. Soon the hospital staff began to train him to be a paramedic. He learned to give injections and to help the nurses treat the other patients. After several years, Bhaskar was pronounced symptom free. Now he could leave the hospital. But where to go? Who would take him in, having had leprosy. He opted to stay on and work in the hospital.

Now the nurse who had admitted him told him that she had found a young lady who was also symptom free and whose family refused to let her come home. Would Bhaskar be interested in marrying Kamala?

Looking shyly at Kamala, Bhaskar related: "She is of high caste background; I wondered if she would have me."

Kamala rejoined, "Leprosy is no respecter of persons. Besides, Bhaskar, as well as I, had found Christ as Savior while being treated. We had a wonderful wedding right on the hospital compound."

"We have had good years since then," Bhaskar added, "with two fine sons and training given us. I went to work for the manager of the hospital; we both served as kitchen workers and helped take care of the small MKs growing up in the home. But now the family was leaving India on furlough, and after twelve years in the hospital we came to you."

Bhaskar and Kamala had become a very integral part of my life. For the last twenty-five years that I served in India, they took full responsibility for helping me with cooking, washing and ironing, and keeping the house clean. In addition, when I was traveling with my books to conventions, Bhaskar cared for the servicing of the car, packing and unpacking my books, witnessing to whomever he could about Christ, and generally making himself indispensable to me. It was during this time that we also began praying for his sons who were maturing rapidly. He was concerned that they not only find Christ but also that they serve Him.

One evening, I heard a rap on my office door and

opened it. There stood little Madhu, Bhaskar's nine-year-old son, barefooted and scared. Assuming that he had misbehaved because he was at my door, I asked, "What did you do?"

He stammered in Marathi (the language I had learned), "I want to be saved."

From my desk I took a small booklet entitled *The Heart of Vijay,* a tract explaining the way of salvation, as Madhu blurted out his story: "During our evening devotionals, my parents were talking about Christ's second coming. I asked my father what would happen to those who had not accepted Jesus as their Savior, and he answered, 'Madhu, your mother and I are concerned for you because unless you accept Jesus, you will not go to be with Jesus when He comes.' This frightened me and I asked him to bring me to you so I could be saved, but he said I had to come on my own. It's been three days since then, and I'm so scared."

Bhaskar had felt that Madhu must come alone; then he would feel that his son was serious about his salvation. That evening I led him to the Lord. I shall never forget his prayer as he asked Jesus to come into his heart. He prayed, "Lord Jesus, don't let those dirty animals be in my heart, but let the dove of peace come in to stay."

Praise God, he came in, and today Madhu is a preacher of the Gospel, having graduated with his M.Div. from Union Biblical Seminary. He is pastoring one of our Alliance churches. He married a lovely Christian girl who is a translator of English manuscripts into Christian Marathi literature with Word of Life Publications. Premdas, the older son, also came to Christ and today is the cashier of Union Biblical Seminary and is married to a Christian nurse. The entire family is serving the Lord. Bhaskar himself assisted our mission in planting a church in one of the large cities of India and became its first elder. He conducts prayer meetings in his home and witnesses to his Hindu neighbors.

When it was time for me to retire from India, I wondered where Bhaskar and his family could live, as he had never earned sufficient money to buy a house or a plot of land, which to every Indian is a necessity. Again, God was not to be outdone. An elderly lady in the United States who prayed for me for a number of years had been also praying for Bhaskar. The Lord put it into her heart to do something for Bhaskar. One day I received a letter from this dear lady, in which she had also enclosed a check for $1300 which she had saved out of her meager pension. She wanted it to go towards the purchase of a small plot of land and house for Bhaskar and his wife when I left India.

There were still two years before I was to leave, and Bhaskar searched for land. Again God gave him favor in the eyes of a rich landlord who sold him property at a greatly reduced rate. For the next two years this dear lady sent checks to pay for the foundation of the house, for the walls, and for the roof. Finally, a lovely little three-room house was completed, largely with secondhand materials which Bhaskar found and purchased for a fraction of their original price. Truly God provided for this healed leper and proved His faithfulness to Bhaskar and Kamala in incredible ways.

When I think of the lives of Bhaskar and Kamala, whom their families deemed "rubbish" and turned out of their homes because of ignorance concerning a dreaded disease, my heart is filled with praise that God redeemed them and made them sons of God and worthwhile citizens, serving Him in gratitude for what He had done for them. Truly they are thankful lepers!

Korea

CAMP MOUNT O PINES IN KOREA

JOHN COOK

John Cook had accepted the Lord only three months before he enrolled at Toccoa Falls Institute. After graduation, he and his wife Lois went to Korea under Child Evangelism Fellowship Inc. in 1957. They served there for 25 years, establishing and building an effective CEF ministry there. Later they directed CEF's ministries in the 15 countries of the Orient and South Pacific. They are now serving at the home office of CEF Inc.

As we served in Korea under Child Evangelism Fellowship in the early 1960's, God showed us a special need among English-speaking children growing up in that foreign land. We wondered how we could reach them with our ministry.

We were friends with most evangelical missionaries who had gone to serve the Lord in this land, which had been ravaged by the Korean War just a few short years before. Among our many missionary colleagues was a man by the name of Robert "Chris" Christopolus, serving under The Evangelical Alliance Mission. God had given Chris a ministry of developing a Christian conference ground in the mountains north of Seoul City, Korea's capital.

Standing together one afternoon, Chris and I were viewing the buildings and grounds God had provided in this beautiful mountain setting. At that moment God spoke to both of us. Would not this be the ideal location for a camping program for children?

We prayed, enlisted other missionaries, and utilized what experience I had had in children's summer camps; and we set out to establish a summer Bible camp for children of missionaries, businessmen, and military personnel. We started from scratch. A name was chosen: "Camp Mount O

Pines."

The first year we were able to develop a camp program for about sixty elementary-age children. The following year we added an additional week of camp for junior high youngsters. Soon Camp Mount O Pines became a yearly three-week program: one week each for elementary, junior high, and high school youth. Camp Mount O Pines was established.

This summer camping program for English-speaking children in Korea continues to this day. By now, literally thousands of children have enjoyed the camp. It is an event that small children look forward to being able to attend "when I get old enough." Parents have even delayed their long-awaited furlough because of their children's desire to be at Camp Mount O Pines. The children do not want to miss their anticipated camp experience.

Most important is the fact that hundreds of children have been saved and have dedicated their lives to the Lord at Camp Mount O Pines. Former campers have come back years later to serve as camp counselors, teachers, and some even as camp directors. It is a Korean missionary institution.

In the same way that Camp Mount O Pines came into being for the English-speaking community of Korea, similar summer camps were introduced into the Korean CEF program and churches through Child Evangelism Fellowship Inc. A number of these camps now own their own property and are members of Christian Camping International.

Praise God that in Korea children are being reached with the gospel through Christian camps like Camp Mount O Pines.

Malaysia

MORE THAN CONQUEROR

REBECCA CARTER EGELER

After graduation from TFC and completion of home service, Rebecca and Bob Carter were assigned to Dalat School as teachers. Following Bob's death, Becky went to The Alliance Academy in Quito. She is now married to Tim Egeler.

It was Canadian Thanksgiving Day, Monday, October 14, 1985, and a holiday at Dalat School on the Island of Penang, Malaysia. The Canadian staff and students were busy making preparations for the special dinner we were planning to have that evening.

Some of the students planned to go bowling in the morning. In the afternoon some were going to the beach and others to the waterfall--about a half hour away. Sponsors were needed to go with the dorm parents, so my husband Bob decided to go with the group going to the waterfall. I took the opportunity to go shopping in the morning and then came home to finish making pies for the dinner.

Neither Bob nor I had been to the waterfall. I thought it was a hiking trip. Had I known there was a small pool above the falls where the kids would swim, I'm sure I would have thought, *This might be the time Bob doesn't come back.* Instead, I didn't give it a second thought.

During our first two years of marriage, I had continually feared for Bob's life. Since we were youth sponsors while in college at TFC, we had outings with the young people, often to Lake Yonah near Toccoa. I'd go with Bob and the group as often as possible; but when I couldn't go, I was sure something would happen to him. Every time when he came home I was relieved.

One day I realized how foolish it was to worry and to think that I had control over what could happen to my husband. I knew this wasn't pleasing to God. Finally I knew I had to give Bob over completely to the Lord to use and to take in His own time. This was not easy, but I prayed that the Lord would prepare me for whatever the future held. I knew that in my own strength I couldn't handle a crisis.

Part of my fear stemmed from three previous tragic events in my life. In my senior year of high school in Quito, Ecuador, a boyfriend had drowned while on a fishing trip with his father. Then in college another friend whom I had dated was killed in a motorcycle accident. On November 6, 1977, the dam above the school at Toccoa Falls broke and flooded the campus, taking 39 lives.

Bob and I were engaged at the time and he nearly lost his life early that morning. In fact when he was coming up out of his basement room, he turned to go back down to see if a friend was trapped. As the water was rising very rapidly, another friend grabbed him and so saved his life. I somehow knew Bob was all right before I ever saw him in the morning.

That same night a friend and I had spent several

hours with Margaret Fledderjohann (Pinney) while she waited to hear news of her husband. God gave her, after she learned that her husband was with the Lord, a beautiful testimony of praise and courage which had a lasting impact on my life.

God was answering my prayer by taking away the fear and helping me to reflect on His sufficient grace during these trials. I had also read several books about people's lives and their testimonies through pain and suffering. The Lord gave me real peace and courage.

Bob also had a premonition about his death. I didn't know this until after he had died. The wife of his boss mentioned that Bob had once told them he felt that he wasn't going to live very long. So we both had a sort of silent understanding, having never really discussed our deep feeling about this.

Bob was out to make the most of his days here on earth. At the same time, he had a self-sacrificing spirit. He seemed always to be the first to "run to the rescue." He'd read to young people stories about people who sacrificed their lives for others. He also carried a heavy burden for his unsaved younger brother Randy who was enslaved to drugs. Bob was willing to give his life if that would bring his brother to the Lord.

And so it was that on that Monday morning when Bonnie Adams and Lonnie Godfrey came to my door to inform me that Bob had gone over the waterfall, I knew he was with the Lord.

Because it was the rainy season in Penang, the pool above the falls was high and very rough. Before the sponsors had even arrived at the top, the kids were going in, not realizing the danger. Jenny Persky was immediately carried to the edge. As Bob arrived, he and Virgil Adams saw her and immediately jumped in to save her. Bob got between her and the edge of the falls and in a split second managed to push her up onto a rock--before going over himself. I was told that his face was completely peaceful and calm.

A few days later God's will and plan for Bob's life was made even clearer in my mind through a dream. Wayne Peterson, the dorm father for the junior high girls, had dreamed the night before the tragedy that someone went over the waterfall and into the arms of God. The next morning Wayne almost told the director his dream so the trip would be canceled. Then he decided not to, figuring that it was only a dream. This dream became very special to me and a great comfort to my heart during times of doubt and uncertainty. Though I had accepted Bob's death, I would still ask "Why?" many times.

I shall always be grateful to the faculty, staff, and students at Dalat for the prayer, love, and support they gave Kristi (our daughter), Bob's family, and me during those days and months of grief. One student fasted and prayed for three days. Another made a pillow for me and a wall hanging for Kristi. A third wrote out scripture verses and placed them in a New Testament. The school staff put together for Kristi a beautiful wood-carved album with pictures and letters from students about her Daddy. The national staff brought us food and told us how much Bob's friendship had meant to them.

And I'm thankful to all our friends at Toccoa Falls and in Florida and around the world, many of whom I had not met, who prayed and wrote to us.

Probably the most important lesson that I have learned is that prayer really makes a difference in our lives. I have also learned to accept God's timing of events in my life, knowing that "His ways are higher."

Mary Kadle, a friend who lost her husband on the mission field, once said to me, "In acceptance lieth peace." I have never forgotten that statement. We can choose bitterness which will destroy our spirit, or acceptance which will give peace.

Our years at TFC provided a wonderful foundation for our trust and faith in the Lord. Though it was a difficult time for the college, God used the tragic event of the flood to fulfil His purpose for the school and for individual lives. In the same way, many lives were affected through Bob's death.

While at Toccoa Falls I chose my life verses, Romans 8:37-39: *But in all these things we overwhelmingly conquer through Him who loved us. For I am convinced that neither death, nor life, nor angels, nor principalities, nor things present, nor things to come, nor powers, nor height, nor depth, nor any other created thing, shall be able to separate us from the love of God, which is in Christ Jesus our Lord* (NASB).

Thailand

EVEN TO THE SMALLEST DETAILS!

DEBORAH ECKMAN

Deborah Eckman grew up as an MK in Irian Jaya. After a year at TFC, she transferred to Brenau, where she earned her R.N. degree. She recently completed a term of service with CAMA Services in Thailand.

CAMA Services has a multinational medical team working among the Cambodian displaced persons along the Thai-Kampuchean border. Because of the cross-cultural nature of overseas mission work, one involved in such situations is confronted daily by unanticipated frustrations and barriers to becoming "one" with the host population. In addition, the person working among displaced and refugee populations must face daily emotional stress when realistically assessing the people's hope for a "normal" future. The conflict and dilemmas of refugee life become the norm as hope lies dormant in the memories of adults. The children are left with mere dreams as they try to imagine life beyond the restrictive barbed-wire fences of their confines.

It was in such a setting that I was involved overseas. Long days, the relentless heat of Thailand,

and the bleak realities of the Cambodian situation had changed my image of "missionary life" and had pressed my faith to the limit. The long lines of persons seeking medical care in the camp's outpatient department (OPD) and emergency admission area were rapidly exhausting everyone's last store of emotional and physical reserve--national and expatriate care-givers alike.

It was my privilege to become friends with the two CAMA Services nurses who directed the daily operations in the OPD: Christa, who had been a Christian for a number of years, and Ingrid, whose Christian walk was substantially newer. Both of these women were displaying near exhaustion under the energy-draining daily scenarios.

The pressures of the moment were awakening in Ingrid the realization that the Lord had promised to bring us no more than we could handle. Committing even the OPD's daily census (number of patients seen) to Him would be an uplifting experience for us. It would also be an opportunity for the Cambodian health care workers to witness God's power at work. This conviction was reconfirmed when Ingrid's daily devotional reading brought her to the passage of scripture in Genesis 24, the account of God's directing Abraham's servant in his search for a bride for Isaac.

"If God could answer that servant's prayers, He surely can help us," Ingrid declared one night. We had just completed another long enervating day in the camp OPD, a day in which we had seen at least 500 patients in a facility staffed to handle about 300 persons maximum. Ingrid continued, "Christa, what do you think would be a realistic and manageable census for the OPD staff to handle in one day?"

The stress that months of burden bearing and suffering had etched on Christa's face deepened. She thought a moment. "About 260," she softly hazarded.

"That sounds reasonable," Ingrid agreed, "but I don't feel I have the strength nor faith myself to make such a request of the Lord. That's about half as many as we've been treating daily. And that with about half our staff working."

"Yes, I know that many are exhausted or ill, or the sickness of family members is keeping them away from work. Yet you asked me, and I still feel about 260 people are all we should have to handle each day."

At that moment Ingrid turned to me. "Will you pray in faith that God will limit tomorrow's census?" she asked. Although I had always given oral assent to God's interest in every aspect of our daily lives, in honesty, my faith was also weak. Yet I was privileged to be asked and challenged to put time in prayer behind my prior spoken trust in God's power. I agreed.

The following day in the OPD seemed to proceed much as all the previous days. The census recording staff was as busy as usual, noting each person who sought medical attention. At the day's conclusion, everyone present was fatigued.

Christa recorded on a piece of paper the number 260. Meanwhile, Ingrid had the Cambodian OPD medical supervisor total the day's census. Ingrid turned to us with a joyful, almost unbelieving look on her face: "The number of people seeking medical attention today is 257!" she cried. "God has answered our prayers; oh, praise Him!"

As a result of these prayers in faith, Christa's endurance was stretched; her faith challenged to be stronger. Ingrid and I were both encouraged as we realized that God had worked in response to our step of faith. The best result, though, was the testimony this situation became before the Cambodian national staff. They had seen the Almighty God deign to stoop down and answer the prayers of three tired Christian nurses. Here truly was a glimpse of the God who attends even to the day's smallest details!

Viet Nam

YAHA, PRINCE AMONG MEN

C.G. INGRAM

C.G. and Jackie Ingram, 1954 graduates of TFC, married in 1957. In 1959 they went to Viet Nam as C&MA missionaries. Forced out by the Viet Nam War after two terms, C.G. has been a pastor since then in the United States.

Born in the jungles of the Roglai people in Viet Nam, YaHa was disowned by his parents early in life. Partly raised by his grandmother, who mistreated him, he became a virtual slave, forced to do all her manual labor.

Surely there is more to life than this, he thought, *but what?* No missionaries had ever been to their tribe; their language was unwritten; YaHa had no one to whom he could go. At this point he met some tribal people who had learned how to read and write.

YaHa thought this was the greatest thing he had ever heard. People could actually learn to read and write! *I want to do that,* he thought and immediately began making inquiries. "Where is there such a school?"

"Oh, it's up north. Missionaries are there, teaching in another language, forget it," he was admonished.

Determined to learn to read and write, YaHa at length found one of these short-term Bible schools and enrolled. First, he had to learn to read and write in the KoHo language which was absolutely different from his native tongue, Roglai, not even in the same family of languages. He determined to learn the KoHo language, and he did!

While in Bible school, he learned about a Savior, Jesus Christ, and put his trust in Him. He wanted to serve Christ. A few years later he met a young KoHo girl who loved the Lord, and they were married. Her brother was pastor of a thriving church; YaHa and his bride moved to this tribe and began assisting in the services. God's blessing fell on YaHa tremendously as he worked, using the KoHo language.

At this time, because of the war situation in Viet Nam, the Vietnamese government began moving the Roglai people who were caught between the South Vietnamese and the North Vietnamese Communists. No one knew exactly what side the Roglai were supporting. Were they aiding and abetting the Communists? The government leaders decided that the best thing to do would be to move them out of the mountains into a new area in a program called Strategic Hamlet. Hosts of people were moved there, not just to keep them in, but to keep the Communists out. Guards protected them.

It so happened that the Roglai people were removed and resettled in the area in which Jackie and I were working. God gave us a real burden for them. We began to study their language, desiring to reduce it into writing so we could give them the Word of God in their own tongue. We knew we were inadequate. We had had a year of Vietnamese, but most of these people could not speak Vietnamese.

Our solution in trying to communicate with them seemed to be to contact YaHa, who we knew was also Roglai, and to ask him if he'd be willing to come and work with these, his own people.

"I don't know," he protested, "God is blessing my ministry here with the KoHo. I am enjoying working with my brother-in-law. I don't really want to change."

"Well, YaHa," I encouraged, "do me a favor. Just come down to our house and we'll go out to the village. We'll see them, talk to them, and then you let the Lord direct you to what He would have you do."

He agreed, and as he went out into the village, the *first* person he met was his old grandmother who had mistreated him and from whose home he had fled years before and whom he had not seen since. During the intervening years he had prayed for her and wondered what had happened to her.

Now YaHa realized that these were not just Roglai people: many of them were his blood relatives. At this point God didn't have to do much speaking to YaHa; he *wanted* to come. His people needed him in many areas of their lives. There were many political problems confronting them, but they desperately needed food and clothing. We tried to help them as best we could.

YaHa straightway began to preach; the church was full. Soon a big church was built, one hundred fifty coming to services and many of them finding Christ as their Savior, including the old grandmother.

When she passed away, YaHa gave her a Christian burial, the first that these people had ever attended. They heard that they need not sorrow or have no hope. YaHa told them about Christ: how He cared for them, that their bodies were in the grave but their souls were with Christ. He was a powerhouse for God; he really had unusual faith and trust in Him.

I often wondered, *Lord, what's so different about this young man? Why is it that the power of God just seems to flow through him; why is he having such a tremendous ministry?*

One day he was in our home with several other preachers; we were making plans for some services. My wife fixed a meal, and we sat down to eat. I noticed that YaHa ate just a small amount, and I

101

encouraged him, "YaHa, eat some more."

"No, it's very good, but you know, at our place we don't have much to eat." He went on, "Sometimes we're hungry, but if I eat very much here, if I just stuff myself, then it'll kind of stretch my stomach, and when I get out in my village and we don't have this kind of food and this much, then I'll be hungry."

That really spoke to my heart and then, just before the meeting ended and I was going to take him back home, we had a time of prayer; and in that time I found the secret of YaHa's ministry and power.

YaHa began to pray; he said, "Lord, I don't really need food. (And I can honestly say that many times in that village they were hungry. I received box cars of relief food to help them. Some of the Roglai actually starved to death because we couldn't adequately feed them. Yet there he was, saying, *I don't need food.* He went on:) It's not clothing I need. (And all the clothing he wore came out of missionary barrels sent over by people in the States. Oh, he looked all right; that's what he had, and he said, *It's not clothing I need.* Then he added:) It's not money I need. (I thought, *Wow!* When his grandmother passed away, he came to me, saying, "Missionary, I want to give my grandmother a Christian burial, but I don't have the money for a casket [just a wooden box]." We gave him the money needed. Now he was saying, *Lord, I don't need money.* Then God smote my heart when he prayed:) Lord, what I really need is your Holy Spirit in my life so that I can preach the Word to my people so they can come to know Jesus."

This was the secret of his power!

While we were on furlough in 1964 we

received a letter telling us that YaHa had contracted typhoid fever from bad water and had died and gone to heaven. Why was this chosen vessel called home? I don't know, but I'm looking forward to seeing YaHa some day, for I know that he was a man who loved God.

I appreciate the training that my wife and I received at Toccoa Falls that compelled us to go to Viet Nam in order to help others so that they, too, could know Christ; and one day when that great host of people from every tongue, tribe, and nation will stand before God, we're going to share a part of it, and Toccoa Falls College will have a part in that celebration because of what was done there for Jackie and for me--and for all the others who have attended Toccoa Falls College and have gone out to share the message of salvation at home and around the world. It has been our joy to "go to far-off lands."

Viet Nam

WITH THE KATU IN VIET NAM

LEROY JOSEPHSEN

LeRoy and Nancy Josephsen have served the Lord in Viet Nam for 17 years and in the Philippines for 13 years. They have engaged in various ministries throughout the years, including refugee ministry. They anticipate returning to the Philippines.

We were excited; after a year of studying Vietnamese, we were assigned to reach the mountain tribal people called the Katu, numbering about 30,000 people. So Nancy and I moved from Da Nang up into the mountains into the Katu tribal area. From our mission house we could look east toward the China Sea, where lived Vietnamese-speaking people, then to the west up into the jungles and over into Laos, the portion inhabited by the Katu.

The Katu were considered the most fierce of all groups in Viet Nam. Once a year they offered a human blood sacrifice to their gods: a Frenchman (since the French soldiers had not treated them well) or a lowland Vietnamese, or even a lower Katu tribal person. Because of their religious beliefs, they believed that they must offer a blood sacrifice to their gods.

Our first task was to learn the Katu language, which is very different from Vietnamese. Since it had never been written, it was our responsibility to try to write it down so that the people could learn to read and speak it; and then, as time would go by, we'd be able to translate some scriptures.

We hiked up to the first village (the only means of travel), seeking a helper. We finally found a Mr. Nam, who agreed, "I will come to your house once a day and help you to understand my language." He added, "I will come if there's no flooding, if there's no rain, and if no one is sick in our village." He added a number of other conditions.

We were thankful that he did come a couple of times a week. He would get very tired of working with me and get up to wander through the house. He'd look through all the rooms, closets, and even drawers. "What is this? What is that?" he would ask. This gave us an opportunity to try to converse in Katu.

After we learned some Katu, we would hike up into the jungles, going into the different tribal villages preaching the Gospel. Oftentimes, when we got near a village, I would take out my trumpet and play some song. The people in the fields would then say, "Oh, the missionary has come." They would assemble in the village, and we could preach the Gospel to them.

Our language helper, Mr. Nam, enjoyed showing visitors around our house, as it was extremely different from theirs. He'd show them the big mirror, and they would look inside their mouths and be astonished to see themselves. Then Mr. Nam would take them to the shower and say, "If you turn this handle, it will rain on you." Everyone would be very surprised to see it rain inside a house. In the bathroom he would say, "Now, you see this pipe here. After you finish here, you pull this handle and then everything will go down to Hell." Quite a novel way to explain a flush toilet!

When people would come, Nancy would give them some tea to drink and put a cube of ice in it. The people had never seen ice. They'd call their tea hot, and then hold the ice in their hands and say, "Oh, this is very hot." They'd call it a "hot rock." They'd say, "What shall I do with my 'hot rock'?"

Nancy would answer, "Just throw it away," but

they'd put it in their pockets.

Soon they'd ask, "Why is my pocket all wet? Where is my hot rock? Where is my hot rock?"

We were dealing with a group of people who had not been out of the jungles; it was a challenge for us to take the Gospel of Jesus Christ to them.

As time went by, the Communists--the Viet Cong --began to infiltrate our area. The government told us, "You cannot go out at night anymore, and at dark you must lock your windows and doors and stay inside." With no electricity we went to bed and arose early. Each evening we would see the different groups of Viet Cong in their black pajamas. On many occasions they would go to the Vietnamese villages east of us and arrest and kill people.

One evening a secret policeman came to our house. He was from the government of Saigon. He acted very, very frightened and very nervous. He said to me, "Missionary, I want to show you something." He showed me a little black notebook. I looked at it and it had *everything about me:* what I did every day, where I went, how much rice I gave out to people, how much salt I gave, sermons I had preached, people who had been saved, those names of tribespeople who had received Christ as Savior, those we had baptized. It was all in the book.

You could have asked me, "Roy, what did you do yesterday or the day before?" I would not remember, but it was all there in the book. It was really frightening.

I asked, "Where did you get this book?"

He replied, "The other night we killed a Communist a few hundred yards from your house. Now, missionary, you cannot stay here much longer, but you definitely must close your doors and windows every night and not allow a soul to get inside."

Nancy and I were very worried about the situation. One night when our dog began barking and barking, we were frightened and wondered what we should do. The dog continued to bark; people came closer and closer--we could hear talking and whispering.

Before long the persons were up on our front porch. I slipped to the door and peeked out through a crack and saw someone's hair. I heard someone saying in Vietnamese, "We know he is inside." I continued to listen, and as they would not go away, I called in Vietnamese, "Who is there?"

A person outside answered, "I'm here, Doi."

"Who are you?"

Again he responded, "I'm here, Doi. I have something for you." (Usually when they say something like that, that means from the enemy.) "Open the door."

"I will not open the door. What do you have for me?"

"A letter." After a time they slid the letter under the door. It was from a missionary far to the east and south of us. It read: "Roy, can you please help us? We have a Katu tribal lady who's been in labor for 36 hours. She is going to die if you do not come to help us immediately."

I asked Nancy, "What should I do?" We prayed, then decided that this time, at 10 o'clock at night, I would open the door to these strangers and get into my Jeep to go look for this missionary. When I found the lady, I put her into my Jeep and went on to the city of Da Nang. As I traveled the jungle highway toward Da Nang, I could feel the eyes of the Viet Cong upon us; surely they would shoot us. We prayed all the way and finally arrived in Da Nang at 2 o'clock in the morning. The baby was born in the Jeep. It was dead, but the woman lived.

Later many tribespeople came to our house. We

had not known that the woman whose life we had saved was a chief's wife, but many came to see us and heard the message of the Gospel.

Things got worse as the Communists moved in in 1960, and the government told us, "Missionary, you must move out to a safer place." We had to move back to Da Nang and work from there. We'd go up into the jungles during the day but could not stay overnight. Later we were told: "Missionary, you know the times you walked on the jungle paths, the enemy was as close as touching you. When you stayed overnight in our houses, they stayed in the next house, listening to you. If you had said anything about the Communists, they'd have captured you."

Later, while we were in Hue, a pastor invited me to go to the jungles to preach on a Sunday morning. It was about 65 miles away, the last fifteen miles a dirt road in the jungles. I got to the church on time, but, surprisingly, the people had already started the service and the pastor was getting up to preach.

When I went in and sat down, all the people looked at me as though they had seen a ghost. The pastor asked me, "Missionary, why are you here?"

"Pastor, you invited me, didn't you, to come and preach today?"

"Yes, I invited you, but why are you here?"

I was very much surprised by that question. Then he told me, "Missionary, when you were coming up the highway today on the dirt road, did you see any buses, taxis, trucks, people on bicycles, or anybody walking?"

I answered, "No, Pastor, now that I think about it, I didn't see a soul."

"That's right, Missionary, there's no one using that highway because it was filled the other night with mines by the Communists, and *no one* is driving over that mined road."

I was shocked and surprised, but thankful to God that He had helped me get there safely. Now what should I do? The pastor invited me to preach, and after the service he graciously asked me to lunch, a very delicious meal which I ate in that jungle hideout. I wanted to stay there overnight, but the pastor told me the Communists would be there that night and if they saw me, they'd capture or kill me. "They will also do something to us because they will think we belong to the CIA," he concluded.

In answer to my question, "Where are these Communists?" he pointed them out on the next hill.

We had a very serious prayer meeting. After that, trusting God and again committing my life to Him, I got into my Jeep and drove as fast as I could down that road. I'm sure the angels of the Lord came and lifted that Jeep off the old road, kept it from hitting those mines, and took me back safely to my family.

Nancy and I have driven on roads that were mined: vehicles have blown up in front of us; at other times we have driven across, and vehicles have been blown up behind us. The Lord has definitely been good to us and taken care of us. I want to give Him praise and thanksgiving for what He has done and the way He has blessed our ministry and has kept our family safe. He has seen fit to spare us, and we want to thank and praise Him, and trust that He will continue to use us as we return to the Philippines in the future to serve Him in the years ahead.

Viet Nam

A RACE WITH TIME FOR
THE JARAI NEW TESTAMENT AND PSALMS

CHARLES LONG

Charles and Elma G. (E.G.) Long graduated from TFC in 1957. In the will of God they arrived in Viet Nam in 1958, where they served until they were forced out by the Communists in 1975. Rev. Long is now pastor in the States.

After being radically "born again," I knew instantly that I must see to it that others had access to the powerful Word of God that had raised my life to new heights so quickly and with such great power. Just three weeks later I entered Toccoa Falls Institute to prepare to take God's Word to someone else in the world. That became my life's ambition. It was a straight-arrowed, single-minded vision.

Four years later, in 1957, E.G. and I graduated from Toccoa Falls and went directly to the Summer Institute of Linguistics at the University of Oklahoma. We volunteered for service in New Guinea; however, the C&MA asked us to go to Viet Nam. We arrived there August 16, 1958, and began to learn Vietnamese.

At first Vietnamese seemed a mere barrier to getting to our *real* work of translating the Bible into a tribal language. Soon, however, we began to enjoy Vietnamese with its six tones, the Vietnamese Christians, and their patient efforts that prepared us for service. Rev. Doan-van-Mien was a special friend as he allowed us to accompany him to many congregations throughout Quang Nam province. He let me preach ten minutes in those services. We became fast friends with this worthy, wonderful saint of God who would later become the president of the evangelical church of Viet Nam.

At last *official* Vietnamese language study was over. We were assigned to a tribe. We had helped with a linguistic survey and found there to be twenty-eight tribal languages in South Viet Nam. What excitement there was as we new missionaries fanned out across Viet Nam to reach the tribes! E.G. and I settled into the Jarai tribe at Pleiku.

It was great to be communicating with people in Vietnamese, but we "hit the wall" at Pleiku as the Jarai understood very little Vietnamese. It was back to language learning again. The Jarai were not used to working at a daily hard mental task; therefore, they would teach us for about a month and go back to the village. Four or five teachers would alternate months when they could take our hard driving ambition to learn Jarai. My first attempts to translate scriptures into Jarai were so pathetic that I didn't even try again for some years. Instead we concentrated on preaching, teaching, and conducting leprosy clinics. This practical ministry built vocabulary, grammar, idioms, and familiarity with Jarai form and thought.

As I tell you this, I am aware that I am packing pain, struggle, survival, sweat, despair, spiritual warfare, love, family life, joy, anguish, loss, cross-bearing, Christ-sharing into the smallest of boxes. The lowest point of my life came in the summer of 1962 when I was slowly recovering from a severe case of hepatitis. Three missionaries, Dr. Ardell Vietti, Rev. Archie Mitchell, and Dan Gerber, were abducted at gun point from the Ea Na Leprosarium --and never returned. My wife and two sons escaped that attack by just four nights. Then within a week, she suffered a miscarriage. In extreme physical and mental exhaustion, I was trying to care for our four- and two-year-old sons. *Only God kept me from quitting.*

A desperate and serious young missionary returned from Viet Nam for furlough in July 1963. A vicious war had begun. The Jarai church leader had been murdered by the Communists. I brought home 400 woven bookmarks that said, "PRAY FOR THE JARAI." I gave them only to serious people who promised to pray for the Jarai every day.

The next four years were filled with danger. Thousands would die all around us. In 1968 we would leave Pleiku never to return as long-time residents. However, God began to do great things. The struggling church grew from 100 to over 2,000 believers. We participated in building eighteen buildings. The need for Bible translation haunted me day and night. I was translating, but everything was URGENT. My life was not mine; all seemed out of control. People were suffering, dying, seeking, begging, crying; and they came to our house for help.

The Tet Offensive of 1968 was a horrible turning point. Eight missionary friends were killed. For months no one could live in our houses at Pleiku. More than a thousand were killed just over the west side property line and within sight of the mission houses. My office was destroyed by a plastic explosive charge. I found what had been translated of the book of Matthew on the floor unburned--but trampled, gritty, muddied. Heartbroken and disturbed that I was facing the failure of accomplishing my life's goal, I felt a deep, grim, tight-lipped determination to finish translating the New Testament and the Psalms in the largest Montagnard language of Viet Nam, the Jarai.

It was 1971 before we were able to get back to full-time translation. I made a vow to complete the translation or be killed trying. As a part of the determination, I stopped shaving and vowed to keep a beard as a constant reminder of my only purpose on earth. A Bible study group of about two hundred people, led by Mrs. Davenish, was praying for us, as were the four hundred who took bookmarks, and our home church in Charlotte.

I became a scholar, hermit, recluse; even as I write this, I chuckle, for all my friends know that it would take a personality transplant for me to become any of those things, yet it was essential if the Jarai would ever get the "BOOK." The Jarai helped by protecting me from people who would waste my time. They asked every day: "Oi, when will the 'BOOK' be finished? Isn't the 'BOOK' finished yet? What are you doing?"

On Easter Sunday, 1972, the North Vietnamese assaulted three South Viet Nam cities: Quang Tri, Kontum, and An Loc. They were using tanks and heavy artillery. A shiver went down the collective spine of South Viet Nam. My wife was out of the country helping with a hepatitis epidemic at Dalat School. My two translation helpers returned to their home villages fearing that their families would need them. I was at Cheo Reo alone. Just in case the enemy tried to cut Viet Nam in half at Cheo to Tuy Hue, I packed a duffle bag with malaria pills, a mosquito net, writing supplies, and some clothes. I was determined to finish the translation even if I had to "disappear into Jarai villages" to do it.

The translation team had just finished translating Romans, but I was not satisfied that it was more than technically correct. The book did not read well in Jarai. I began to seek God for His inspiration. As I reread Romans, new ideas began to flow. Since I was alone, nothing--days, nights, mealtimes--hindered constant fellowship with God and with the words of God in Romans. I could hardly wait for our household helper, a Jarai man, to arrive in the morning to go over what had been done during the night. I can imagine what it was like for the writers of the Bible to be inspired by God. It was not work. Sleep came only when I was truly exhausted. The book was in my mind every waking hour, hours filled with the presence of God, conversations with Him, and answers from Him. I do not remember how long it took in hours, days, or weeks. I only remember that it was a highlight of my life and certainly a highlight of my spiritual life.

Romans was then typed in triplicate and distributed to three Jarai to read and critique. Very quickly after it was distributed, one of the readers returned with the book of Romans rolled up in his hand. It looked old, dirty, tattered, used. With tears in his eyes he begged, "Mr. Long, may I keep the book; it has gotten into my spirit?"

My reply was, "Yes, just let me get your corrections first, and then you may have it." Romans was the book that drew emotional reactions. Chapters five through eight had all the power that God intended them to have on all who leave the flesh to walk in the Spirit.

Months were spent in typing "error free" manuscripts for the press. Typesetting with individual pieces of lead type took nine months. The press could set as many as twenty-four pages at once, and then we had to proofread until no errors were found. The final New Testament and Psalms was eight hundred ten pages. Some of the books were done by Rev. Truong-van-Sang, a Vietnamese missionary to the Jarai. The typesetting was completed in June 1974; the finished photo-ready work, given to the United Bible Society in Hong Kong on July 4, 1974. Seven thousand copies were printed and dedicated to the glory of God at the

Pleiku Jarai church on February 16, 1975. *Communist troops overran Pleiku just one month later!*

I never had opportunity to preach from the printed book until I was sent to Bataan, Philippines, in October 1986 to prepare Jarai refugees for entry to the USA. One young Jarai wanted me to see his worn, jungle-dirtied New Testament, a gift from a friend. This young man had received Christ in 1982, seven years after the fall of South Viet Nam. It was breathtaking for me to stand by his side, observe his love for Christ and the BOOK that shared Christ with him. What if, somewhere along the way in the course of the twelve years that it took to do the translation, I had lost the month that was needed to get the BOOK to Pleiku in February before the Communists arrived in March?

Beside my senior photo in the 1957 *Forrester* was written my life ambition: "I want to make it possible for those who have never heard the Gospel to read of God's Son in their own language" (Romans 10:13, 14, and 17).

As a postscript, a pastor who is a recent refugee from the Jarai area of Viet Nam reports that the revival begun in 1971 continues and that the Jarai Christians now number over 27,000!

THE ISLAND COUNTRIES

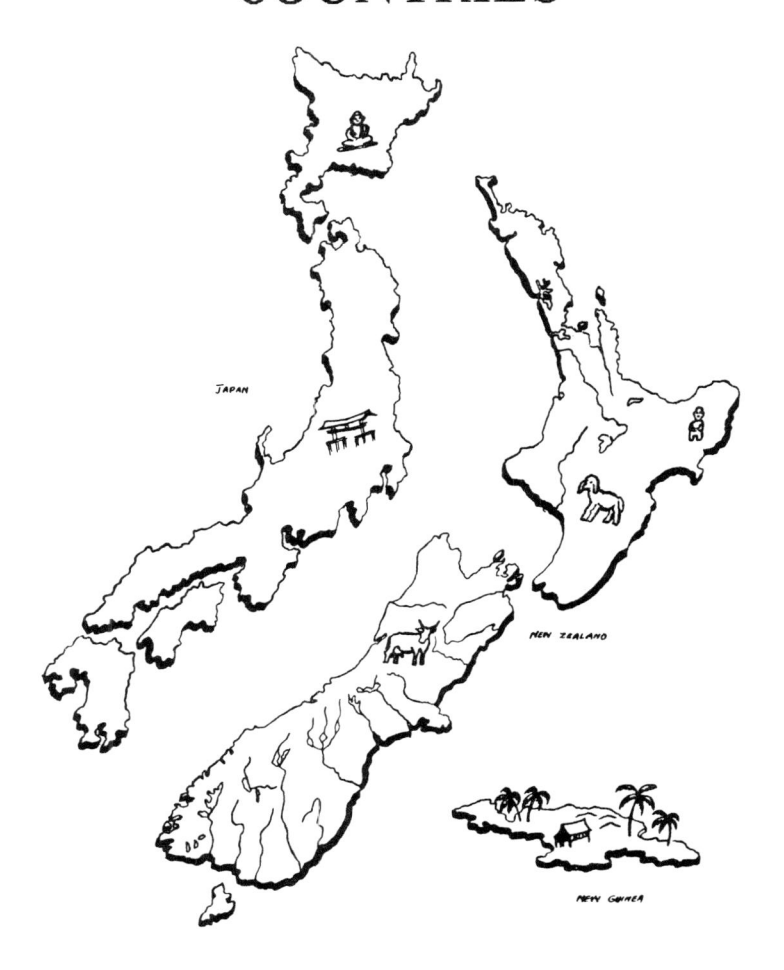

Indonesia

FROM THE OTHER SIDE OF THE WORLD

JUDY GASKIN

In Indonesia since 1971, Judy Gaskin has conducted teacher training classes for Sunday school workers, taught in Jakarta Bible College, and coordinated retreats for teachers of pre-teen Sunday schools.

In Wesley Duewel's book, *Touch the World Through Prayer,* many instances are given of the vital role of prayer in the lives of God's children. As a missionary with the C&MA in Indonesia, I am extremely conscious of the power of intercessory prayer in my behalf by others.

I will never forget the year 1985. I had suffered several bouts of undiagnosed fevers and chills accompanied by terrible headaches. The worst attack was yet to come. As usual, my "undiagnosed sickness" would suddenly begin with a terrible headache followed by high fever and chills. On this particular occasion the fever continued to climb higher and higher. To keep my head from "bursting open," I tied a cotton belt around it.

When the thermometer read 105.5, I knew I needed a divine touch from Him. Between times of hallucinating, I cried out to the Lord, "Lord, please touch me or take me home to heaven; I can't stand it any longer."

Shortly after that call of despair, my fever broke, leaving its mark of a row of "fever blisters" from my upper lip to the tip of my nose. During the next few days I knew I had experienced a "special touch" from Him.

A week later I received from one of His faithful warriors at home a letter that was to reconfirm to me the power of intercessory prayer. This elderly saint of God wrote, "Judy, have you been sick or in some difficulty? I was awakened during the middle of the night yesterday with a 'heavy burden' for you. I felt as if you were in trouble. I got up and prayed for you until the burden was lifted." She proceeded to tell me the exact time and date of that unusual experience.

It was not a surprise to me when I figured out that her burden for me was lifted heavenward to our loving Father at exactly the same time I cried out on the other side of the world for healing or homegoing.

Through the prayer of one of His saints, God chose to touch me with His healing hand "on the other side of the world."

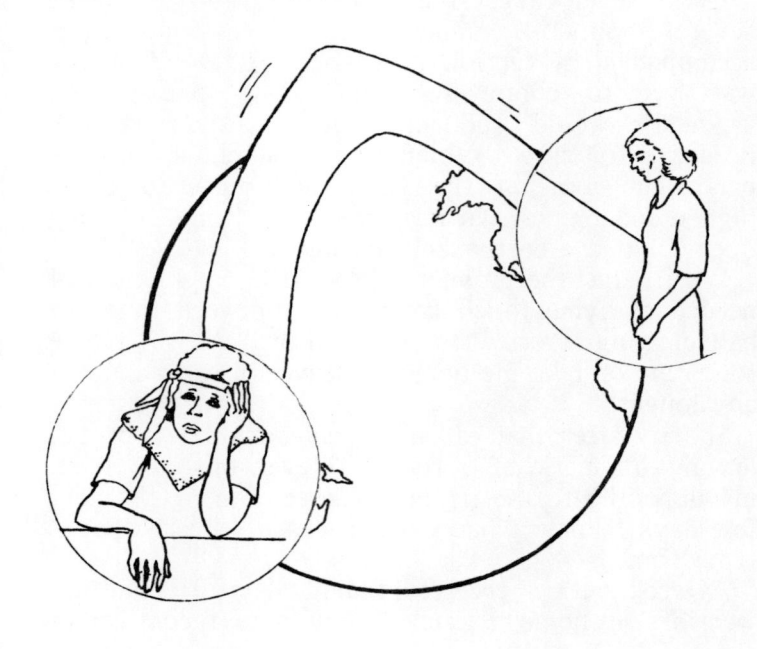

Irian Jaya

"BEFORE THEY CALL, I WILL ANSWER"

CAROLYN ECKMAN

David and Carolyn Eckman went as missionaries to Irian Jaya in 1961. While home on furlough in 1980, David went to Glory. Carolyn had already accepted a position at TFC, working in Student Ministries. There were four children to rear; she remained on the staff at TFC, where she is now Associate Dean of Student Activities and Dean of Women.

When David and I went to Irian Jaya, we had one son, Jonathan, five months old. Packing our things for the next four years included clothing that would be needed for all three of us. How many pairs of shoes would we need for four years? How many pairs of socks, blouses, shirts, dresses, trousers; and what sizes would Jonathan be wearing in the next four years? There was also the question of plates, cups, saucers, kitchen utensils, bed linens, towels, and all supplies for living in a foreign country.

Getting all this together and packed consumed all of our final days before leaving for Irian Jaya. It was a great day when we saw the truck leave our driveway with the drums packed, locked, addressed, and now being shipped to our new home. Even the box containing our bed mattress looked good on the back of that truck.

Several days later we said our goodbyes to family and friends in the Atlanta airport. Our carryon luggage was very heavy and bulky. The diaper bag was overstuffed with all I'd need for the several days of our journey. My purse even held a hammer, as it had been forgotten while we were packing the drums. Even though my shoulders were weighted down, I tried to stand straight as I went down the walkway to the inside of the plane. We sighed with joy and sorrow--joy to be on our way with everything we needed sent, but sorrow to be leaving our loved ones. We brushed away the tears as we thanked God for His leading and provision for us.

Adjustment to life in Irian Jaya went quite smoothly. The folks who met us were wonderful. One of the ladies carried Jonathan for hours as he cried from stomach pain as a result of being given the wrong formula in one of the hotels on the way. The heat was overwhelming for a few weeks, but we acclimated. The lack of water was disturbing for a short time; not understanding the language was frustrating; but this, also, fell into place as we studied the foreign language. All was going well, and we were fitting into our new culture and family.

Only a couple of months later, I began having morning sickness. Sure enough! We were going to have an addition to our family. The heat seemed to intensify; the food became distasteful; but I adapted. As it neared time for our baby to be born, I had one scary question: "What will I do if this is a girl? I have *no clothes* for a little girl." I had brought only boys' clothing.

On August 20, the midwife in the Jayapura hospital announced to me, "You have a fine little girl!" I was overjoyed with this gift from God--but what would I do about clothing for a little girl? I had some diaper shirts to start with, and I just prayed that God would provide.

At that time the stores in Jayapura were empty because of political unrest, and no supplies were available, especially baby clothes. The MAF plane came back from Pyramid station after delivering their goods. The pilot smiled as he handed my husband a large box that had been sent out from the missionary at Pyramid. When we opened the box, we found it full of little girls' clothes, just what I needed! I cried and thanked God for meeting that need.

The following July we were going to our annual missionary conference. On Sundays everyone dresses up nicely. I had selected special clothing for David, Jonathan, and myself, but I had nothing for our precious Susanna. Again I stopped and prayed, "Lord, You know the desire of my heart for a beautiful new dress for our darling little girl. Please, could You give one to me?"

Because I was on the setup committee, I had to take the children and go on into the station where the conference was to be held several days before David could. As I got on the plane, my parting words were: "I love you; pray for a dress."

David laughed as he walked away.

The day of the opening of conference is very exciting. The planes land and take off all day as they bring the missionaries from the whole island in for conference. There is laughing and crying as we meet each other, since many have not been together for a year.

When the plane arrived from Jayapura bringing David to Pyramid, the children and I were there to meet him. The first thing he handed me was a package from Arlington, Virginia. It was from Aunt Pearl. We hurried to the room to open our gift, and in the package were *two little dresses,* size twelve months! They were the most beautiful dresses ever made for a little girl, just the right color, pattern, and size.

Our Susanna became a little doll in those dresses!

The most amazing of all was that the package had been sent *eleven months* earlier from Virginia. As soon as Aunt Pearl had heard of Susanna's birth, she had sent it. Why did she not send six-months' size? Why two dresses, one for each Sunday of conference? Why did the package take eleven months to arrive in Irian? Because God loves us enough to care about the desires of our hearts. Because He knows our needs even before we do and provides even before we ask. Praise God! "Great Is Thy Faithfulness."

I continue to experience this fact today--God loves me and continually meets every need!

Irian Jaya

IHU MAURI'S REQUESTS AND PRAISES

CAROLYN ECKMAN

Missionaries are sent to teach people overseas. Sometimes it is the reverse, and the missionary learns from the people instead. This was the case in Irian Jaya as it happened to Mrs. Eckman.

Ihu Mauri was a lady small in stature and not at all attractive. She began coming to a ladies' Bible study in Irian Jaya as a result of an invitation from one of her neighbors. After several weeks of faithful attendance, she accepted Christ as her Savior. This caused a drastic change in her life.

Ihu Mauri was the mother of eleven children--all boys. Her husband wanted desperately to have a daughter and blamed her for the fact that every time there was another baby born, it was a baby boy. Another strike against her was the fact that four of these sons were albinos. Her husband began to make life miserable for Ihu Mauri. He decided that he would take another wife and bring her into the same house. This did not go well as there was much arguing and fighting. He actually cast Ihu Mauri and her sons aside.

Ihu Mauri had to take the responsibility for all of the food for her sons. Much of her time was spent in the garden, growing their food and extra vegetables to sell at the market place, in order to get money for purchasing rice.

Although her life was hard, she kept coming to Bible study and actually drew much strength from the friendship of the ladies. Many times she testified to direct answers to prayer: "My son was sick last night. I had no medicine or money with which to buy any. I knelt by my son, burning with fever, and prayed. His fever broke, and God healed him completely."

Another time she testified: "I had no money and my rice was completely gone. I went to the garden to pick produce to take to the market to sell. Nothing was ready to harvest. I prayed that God would give me rice to feed my sons. When I reached my home, there was a sack of rice at my back door. I was so thrilled I cried and cried. Then, I took half of the rice and shared it with my neighbor who also was out of food." (What an example to me --the missionary! I'd have used all the rice myself.)

The best lesson of all that I learned from Ihu Mauri was through one of her requests and praises. She had been asking the ladies of the prayer group to pray for her about her lack of control of her temper. Many times she became very angry. We were all praying for her.

Bible study time came again. Ihu Mauri came into the room with welts on her arms and legs. It was obvious that she had again been beaten by her husband. As we shared in testimony, I purposefully skipped her. When the other ladies finished their sharing, I tried to jump into the prayer request time. Ihu Mauri spoke up. "I would like to give a praise."

For what? I thought. *You are all beaten up.*

She continued, "I have been asking you ladies to pray for control of my temper. Last night I asked my husband for money for rice to feed my sons. He became very angry with me and beat me terribly. You can see the marks on my body. I praise God! I did *not* get angry and did not fight back. God helped me to control my temper!"

As the missionary, I was thinking, *If he had beaten me, I would have picked up a piece of firewood and hit him back.* As I drove home, I felt so ashamed that I didn't thank God for my home situation. I was never beaten, but often found myself grumbling. I learned much from Ihu Mauri that day--a lesson I shall keep for life. Praise God for teaching me through a small Irian Jaya lady!

Irian Jaya

ATTENDING A CANNIBAL FEAST

FRANCES BOZEMAN

Thomas and Frances Bozeman in 1956 became two of the earliest missionaries in the Baliem Valley, where they engaged in pioneer evangelism and church planting. Since Tom's death in 1986, Frances has been re-assigned to serve as dietician at Dalat School, Malaysia.

Since we had come to live with the Stone Age people, known as the Dani tribe, we had heard that they were cannibals. Every few days they would come running, dressed in their very prettiest head gear made of cuscus fur and bird feathers, pig tusks through their noses, and pig fat and soot rubbed into their faces. Their piercing yells would penetrate the air for long distances. They were ready to go to battle with their enemies.

Several times, when we saw fires burning, which we knew were not garden beds being burned off, we questioned them: "What are those fires?"

"Oh, we are eating an enemy," they would answer.

We never believed them. For one human being to eat another human being was just too inconceivable to us. However, one day, very early, we were awakened by a knock at the door. There stood a group of warriors who, in a very friendly manner, invited Tom and a fellow missionary, Ed Maxey, to attend a cannibal feast. We knew that they had fought a battle the day before because we had given medical treatment to some of the wounded. At that time they had told us of the victory in killing an enemy.

The missionaries, still unbelieving, agreed to

accompany the warriors, saying as they went out the door, "We are taking our cameras just in case it is true; no one will ever believe us otherwise."

Along the trail they joined other people in a very festive mood, eager to celebrate the victory. This was not unusual, for each time an enemy was killed, they had a victory dance. They ran around in circles, singing and whooping and hallooing. However, they seldom retrieved the body of the enemy because this was too dangerous.

Upon reaching the large field where the celebration was to take place, Tom and Ed saw hundreds of people--men, women, and children--all dancing. It seemed that no one was sitting this one out. Suddenly the excitement became even greater, and the crowd began to make a path in the center.

Tom and Ed were stunned as they saw several men carrying a man tied to a pole. His body was filled with spear holes, and some of the flesh had been scraped off where they had apparently dragged him along the trail. As the warriors carried his body down the aisle, the people would yell insults at him. Then suddenly, from across the gorge came sounds of mourning, crying, and pleading: "Please give us back our body; give us back our friend, our father!"

To these cries the warriors would yell in return, "No, we will not give him back. We are going to eat him!"

Without any warning, the men suddenly pounced upon the dead body and began to cut him as one would butcher a cow. The missionaries stood there, speechless, disbelieving. A fight broke out among the ones who were doing the cutting over who would get what parts. Tom would take pictures, then become so nauseated he would have to leave, only to return for more pictures. Surely no one would believe if there was no proof.

After a while Tom and Ed walked slowly away. Many thoughts disturbed and troubled their minds. Here were people for whom Christ died, not even realizing there was a Savior, much less knowing Him as their very own. "Lord, help us to be faithful to learn the language well, to give them the Gospel, and to illumine their understanding to receive it."

For two or three days the missionaries wanted nothing more than toast and tea to eat. They had no appetite. It was a while before they wanted to talk much of the incident, but one thing that Tom kept telling me was, "I saw a young boy there with such an unusual face. I don't know why he stood out to me, for they all look so much alike, but I want to be faithful to pray for him. His name is Hilitu, and he ate part of the man's stomach."

We were faithful in praying for Hilitu (which means "fire"). Then one day several months later, a small lad appeared at our door and said, "I came to see Tuan Botman (Mr. Bozeman)."

Tom came over to see who it was. Excitedly he said to me, over and over, "This is Hilitu."

Hilitu began to work for us, gathering firewood and sweeping the floor. He lived in a little hut just outside our door, and each night before he went to bed we would tell him a Bible story. I taught him to read from primers; we had no translation of the Bible in his language.

One night before Hilitu left, he said, "Botman, I think I understand about the bad that I have done and that I need Jesus. I want to follow the Jesus road."

That night Hilitu, who had taken part in the cannibal feast, became a child of God.

Irian Jaya

THE GOSPEL INVADES THE BALIEM VALLEY

JAMES SUNDA

James and Deloris Sunda, in 1957, sailed for Dutch New Guinea, where they also became pioneer missionaries to the Baliem Valley. They have engaged in many other ministries since.

Upon our arrival in the Baliem Valley, we spent the first four months living with Tom and Fran Bozeman while studying the language. Then the Field Executive Committee appointed us to open a work in the Wosi Valley. It had been a spot of interest during World War II when an army plane crashed, leaving a WAC and two soldiers as the only survivors. To rescue the survivors, the Army dropped in some men to build a glider strip. In a dramatic operation, the entire ground party was snatched out by gliders.

In preparation for our initial trip to Wosi, Tom Bozeman, Myron Bromley, a Dutch government officer, and I flew to Pyramid, a newly opened station at the opposite end of the valley closer to the Wosi area. There, we hired about a dozen men to help carry our food, sleeping equipment, radio, and other supplies.

After several hours' trek, we crossed the Baliem River and started into the Wosi area. Our destination was the old Army glider strip where we were planning to set up camp for the night. The closer we got to our destination, the more apprehensive our Dani carriers became. They noted that things were not right because we had not met people along the trail, nor had we seen anyone working in the gardens.

"Turn around," they urged us. "Do not go further now; things aren't right!" But we were determined to push on.

We were almost within sight of the glider strip when suddenly our path was cut off by a large group of about 200 Dani warriors dressed in their battle array--their bodies covered with pig fat and charcoal giving them a black sheen, pig tusks hanging through their noses, their hair decorated in long, greasy, shiny curls, and each man carrying either a spear about 15-18 feet long or a set of bow and arrows. They began shouting for us to turn around and leave.

Myron Bromley, our Alliance linguist, was the only one of our party who knew the language well. He began trying to negotiate with them and to explain why we had come. "We have medicine to treat your disease of crippling yaws. We have gifts for you, presents for your chiefs--steel axes, mirrors, red cloth, cowrie shells--see!" We knew these were trading goods they all longed to own to enhance their stature in the community.

They, nevertheless, stood firm in their resolve that we should return to Pyramid. When we didn't cooperate, two warriors jumped up onto the fence and began frenetically rattling their arrows against their bows, inciting the other warriors to action against us. As if they were one body, the entire group of warriors gave a blood-chilling shrill hoot that continued with screeches and screams such as we'd never heard in our lives. To enforce their determination that we leave, they began shooting arrows and throwing their spears right at our feet.

Realizing that there was no reasoning with them then, Myron said, "Let's not panic now, fellows. Let's just turn and start moving off slowly."

However, as the arrows and spears came closer and closer, Tom shouted to me, "Jim, we're going to get killed if we don't get OUT of here!" So we began running for our lives.

We soon had to cross a small ravine with only a single slippery log over it. While crossing, Tom slipped off and fell down into the ravine. As we tried to get Tom out, Myron spoke words of assurance that the Lord was with him. Tom's reply to Myron was, "Yeah! I believe the Lord's with me, but I want Him to be with me up there on the trail, not down here in this hole!" We all had to laugh a little as we ran on.

To assure that we wouldn't stop our flight, the Dani warriors started shooting their arrows closer and closer--so close that one arrow went right through Myron's shirt. One spear hit Tom's boot. Some of them were throwing heavy sticks and big rocks; all of us were hit with some of their better aims. I was hit hard in my lower back with a large rock.

On arrival at the river, as we were getting a raft ready to cross, most of the warriors dispersed, with only a few guarding to insure that we did leave. As we trekked on into the night, hoping to get back to Pyramid, my back began hurting so much that I felt I could not go on. I urged the other fellows to leave me, but they stopped and Tom and Myron prayed for me. As they prayed, the Lord touched me, and all the pain left. We were able to get home that night.

On several occasions we attempted to go into the area, and each time the people threatened to kill us and either stole or tried to steal all of our equipment. Eight years were to pass before we'd be able to get back into that area.

When we were able to reach them, we asked some of the people why they had not wanted us in their area. They told us the story of the US Army crash and of the party who lived with them. They'd cared for them, giving them food and helping them out with a place to stay. Then the Army people had left. Soon an epidemic hit their pigs and thousands of pigs died. They reasoned that their ancestral spirits were expressing their displeasure that they'd entertained the white men in their area, so they brought sickness on their pigs.

When we asked them why they had not just killed us when we came, they answered, "We had never killed a white person before, and did not know how to appease your ancestral spirits. We knew you were powerful people--you knew the source of cowrie shells, you had steel axes and mirrors, you talked into a black box and it talked back to you, you had huge birds that came at your bidding, and you could climb into them and they'd take you places and bring you back again--all of this we observed, and we were afraid of your spirits, so thought it best just to chase you away." We praised the Lord for that!

In the following three years we were in danger many times as we tried to contact the Wosi and other unreached people in the Baliem area. While the Pyramid people, no longer considered hostile, seemed uninterested in the Gospel, the Damal and Dani people of the Ilaga Valley, some one hundred miles northwest, were responding to the Gospel in unprecedented numbers. Soon there were hundreds who had burned their charms and fetishes that they felt connected them with their ancestral spirits. They wanted to follow "The Jesus Way."

As more and more Danis turned to the Lord, Dani people everywhere were very much concerned. In their world view, their fetishes controlled their universe, and if these common fetishes were destroyed, the universe would collapse. They strongly believed that through their fetishes and the sacrifice of pigs, their ancestral spirits were appeased and the spirits, in turn, made their pigs and gardens grow and didn't send sickness and death.

Men were sent to the Ilaga Valley. Upon their return, they reported that the people in the Ilaga Valley were not getting sick and that, in fact, there had been no deaths for two years and that their gardens and pigs were prospering even though people had burned their fetishes and were now following the Jesus trail. They exhorted the people to burn their fetishes and follow the Jesus trail. They cried out, "We should all go to the missionaries and let them teach us the way of eternal life."

An evangelistic party visited other Dani areas; large crowds gathered; in most places the people made commitments to follow Jesus by burning their charms and fetishes. At Pyramid 8,000 to 10,000 people gathered each day to hear the Word of God. On the sixth day group after group of singing people descended on the mission station, bringing their fetishes and firewood. After a preaching service, the people stood to their feet with a loud shout and began preparing the wood as they do for a funeral pyre, then laid on it their nets full of fetishes. Some opened their nets and revealed in their fetishes ancient dog teeth, rat bones, small stones, and even their ceremonial bow and arrow sets used to assure success in battle.

What a sight it was as some 5,000 people made their first commitment to follow the Lord! The following day 3,000 more came to burn their fetishes. It was a tremendous experience.

Through the years God has sent some very talented linguists to work with the C&MA in Irian Jaya. They have reduced to writing the languages of the interior peoples and have translated the Word of God into quite a number of those languages. Other folks with very little training, but with God's help and His wisdom, have translated scriptures for various tribes. Deloris was one of the latter group.

After attending an SIL literacy course, Deloris got the idea that she could make a program that could change a whole sub-language to another sub-language. She was helped and encouraged by an SIL worker who did not tell her that at that time this had never been done before.

The result was that, after many months of frustrating and demanding work, she had a program that, when a diskette with the mid-Valley dialect scriptures was entered into the computer and her changes table was also entered into the computer, she got a readable text in the Wosi dialect. Following that initial effort, it took 3½ years of revising and checking--revising and rechecking--before the New Testament was completed.

The amazing result is that in only four years the entire New Testament was translated into yet another language of Irian Jaya!

Today the work of church planting and of theological education continues. There are now over nine hundred churches in Irian Jaya, all pastored by their own national pastors. These churches are divided into thirty church districts--all having their own district committees, which are, in turn, overseen by an Irian Jaya-wide church president and his committee.

It has been a joy to work with this national church and see God raise up evangelists and church planters who have gone out and evangelized many other valleys and even out into hostile low-land areas. It has been our privilege to help "give light to the blind!"

Japan

SHARING THE WORD WITH RUSSIAN SEAMEN

SUE BENEDICT

Paul and Sue Benedict were missionaries in Japan from April, 1952, to March, 1990, with Southern Baptist missions. For the past twenty years Paul engaged in Harbor Evangelism.

"While they're out of here, I'll hide one of these Gospels under this slipcover where they'll find it later," I whispered to Paul. It was a Sunday afternoon and our family was being entertained on a Russian freighter in port in Yokohama.

The day before, Paul, who did Harbor Evangelism in Japan, had made arrangements for this visit; he had promised to bring his family. So here we were-- the four girls, Paul, and I--seated in the warm sunny mess hall that was used by the ship's officers. On comfortable slipcovered chairs, we sat around a long table covered with fresh linen.

As I nervously pushed the little Russian Gospel of Matthew under the cover of my chair, a Russian seaman entered, bearing a tray of tea and cookies. Very coarse, light-brown sugar sweetened our tea which was served in glasses that rested in little-handled metal holders.

Several men came in to see us; perhaps they were

curious to see who the ship's guests were; more than likely the four young ladies, our daughters, must have made us popular!

A rather halting conversation took place since English was not their native tongue, nor Russian ours. We were impressed with their kindness, though, as they presented us with chocolate bars from their country.

We wondered: *Where are the hostile Russians we Americans have been taught to avoid and fear?* Certainly not on this U.S.S.R. ship; here we were not unwelcome, at least so it seemed. Our new friend, the ship's doctor, was especially genial. There was no sinister look in his warm eyes; he just had an interest in us, an American family. Most likely we were the first Americans he had ever met. After some small talk and inquiry about his family and hometown, we knew that since we were now alone, our opportune moment had come.

Paul, as a harbor evangelist, had been visiting U.S.S.R. ships for almost a year and a half when we had this encounter. At first he had been reticent, then became more and more bold as we found that the Russians, too, were people with problems, joys, and sorrows. Russians were friendly; even members of the dreaded K.G.B. visited in our home. Working with them in Seamen's Mission work had enabled us to become acquainted with their way of life. They showed us pictures of their wives and pretty round-faced children. Hometowns were pointed out on maps. We saw glimpses of loneliness on sad, empty faces and felt their discontent with conditions at home. In Russia, apartment life is crowded and noisy with two families using a common kitchen and bathroom. A Russian only dreams of having his own apartment with private facilities.

At that time church services in underground and

unregistered churches were broken up by the secret police. Christian workers there were beaten and their precious Bibles and songbooks destroyed or taken away from them. Neither pornography nor Bibles were legally owned in Russia; according to the law, both were equally dangerous to the people. The only Bible some Christians possessed was one that had been painstakingly copied down in longhand.

This knowledge had given Paul a burning desire to help the Christians of that land. God had a plan by which He wanted to do the work. Miraculously a large supply of Russian Bibles and songbooks had come to us. We knew God wanted these Bibles given out in Yokohama. Our plan was to get the Bibles out, a few at a time, by contacts with the Russian seamen who came into the harbor on freighters and fishing and passenger ships.

Frequently the seamen were seen in downtown Yokohama, large-boned, conspicuous foreigners among the small Japanese. Invariably they had to travel in groups of three or four, sent out to spy on one another. Carrying large black briefcases, the men stowed away their carefully purchased articles: luxuries such as nylon hose and scarves, lipstick and ballpoint pens. Articles that are very inexpensive in one country can yield a small fortune in another. A Bible was worth from $80.00 to $100.00 on the black market.

"I have an interesting book you may enjoy having," said Paul, approaching the doctor.

"Oh, but sir, I've been on this ship only a short while. . . ."

His reply indicated to us that he was not yet fully established in his own place on this ship, or that perhaps the K.G.B. leader of the Communist party on the ship was a feared man.

"But this book is very valuable," Paul smilingly

volunteered.

"Well, let's take a tour of the ship and then take some pictures of your family," suggested the doctor in a friendly manner.

One by one we followed him, climbing up the narrow steps to the wheel house. The intricacies of the radar system, navigating equipment, and radio room were explained. Strange lettering formed Russian words on the polished wooden doors. Tile floors were scrubbed clean, and brass fixtures shone brightly. But our real mission was as yet not completed.

As we descended the stairs before leaving the ship, a sternfaced seaman came to Paul demanding, "Did you leave this in my room? Here, I cannot take such a book." He returned a Bible that Paul had earlier left in the man's open-doored stateroom.

Now they know who we are! I thought nervously. "Oh, Lord," I prayed, "give us protection and wisdom."

Since the doctor had apparently not seen this exchange, I breathed a prayer of thanks as we continued out to the gangway and down off the ship where we were going to have pictures made.

"Oh, thanks, Doctor, for the nice visit, the tour and all. We had a good time today and would really like you to have this," said Paul, dropping a small green-backed Bible into the doctor's coat pocket.

We lined up for a picture, then climbed into our station wagon. The doctor smiled to us as he waved us a happy goodbye. We believe that he was glad to get the Book, one that can "tickle a Russian pink."

This is not an isolated instance, for we have made many contacts through the seamen. On one occasion Paul was able to rendezvous with a ship officer who was smuggling Bibles into his country. As they met at a designated bookstore, the pickup was made. As the officer stood at the shelves looking at books, his interest was not there, but in the *valuable* books that were being brought to him. And they were free!

In the men's restroom twenty copies of the Russian Bibles and songbooks were deftly transferred into the copious black bag. Having fulfilled their purpose, they would exit, leaving the store in different directions.

Dangerous? Yes, but God enabled and protected His servants. We praise Him!

Japan

DETERMINING TO TRIUMPH

GEORGALYN WILKINSON

Georgalyn Browne Wilkinson lived, as a youngster, on the Far East Broadcasting Company compound in the Philippines. In 1959 she and her husband began their service with F.E.B.C. in Okinawa, later being transferred to Japan. She was also a correspondent for the Foreign Press Association. Since 1986 she has been executive director for GLINT (Gospel Literature International).

It was in Japan at four twenty-eight on Monday afternoon of August 30, 1971, that it was given to me. It was not mine to consider whether or not to accept it, but within a matter of hours God very quietly let me know that my life would be falling into a new category. In the past I had been able to put a check mark beside "Single" and then later, in 1958, I could check the category of "Married."

Now, very suddenly, a new category was mine. Now my check mark would be "Widow." It nearly took my breath away to realize with what speed God had turned my life upside down. Soon He would begin to show me that He had very specific and carefully made plans for my life that until now I had no idea were taking place.

In the weeks that followed, God was closer to me than I had ever permitted Him to be. A new relationship was formed between the two of us that is far too intimate for me to put into expression. That relationship continues to this day, and I pray it will always be so precious.

During those early weeks of adjustment, I tried to listen to the loving advice from many friends on both sides of the ocean. And I realized that I had two very precious daughters, six and eight years old, who needed a whole mother. A healthy, joyous, on-top-of-it-all, in-love-with-Christ mother. I wanted to be that mother to my girls.

As the months went by, we found our little family more in love with each other and with Christ than we had ever been. There was not a day of defeat or depression. As springtime came, we signed up with the Christian Academy PTA charter group to go to the States for our summer furlough, at the end of our three-year term with the Far East Broadcasting Company in Japan. Everything was quite on schedule.

I wondered what the experience of a summer furlough would be without a husband. When we arrived in early June, I remember well the grab in the bottom of my stomach when the keys of the car were handed to me, and I realized that the thousands of miles would be *my* responsibility. All of the setting up of schedules for deputation would also be mine. A flood of *Am I up to it?* thoughts came over me. I know I must have swallowed hard and looked into the face of Jesus, as I so often do, and He knew that I knew that He had to do it. I couldn't.

With the Lord's direction, we were soon sailing along the expressway, the turnpikes, the small lanes, and narrow roads. There were many meetings, and as a novice, all I could do was to share what God meant in my life and how much I wanted Him to be seen to those I loved in Japan.

Weeks passed. We were delighted with America, with our friends, with visiting relatives. It was a time of assuring them, too, that we really were all right, as we had said in our letters from Japan. God had done a work in our hearts.

Toward the end of summer--it happened to be on my birthday--on August 18, we were staying at a Holiday Inn in Phoenix, Arizona. It was the first birthday for me without David's doing something very, very special for me. But this day was different. We were traveling. Strangers in the city. My thoughts turned to Dave and to our girls, Barra and Janel; I recall looking into the mirror as I was brushing my hair that special night in my life and stopping suddenly and wondering, *Oh, am I falling into the luxury of tears? Am I going to permit myself to fall into comfortable depression? Can it be that after all these months when God has walked with me in every footstep that now the memories of the year would flood through my heart and soul so that I couldn't breathe?*

Knowing that God intended things to be exactly as they were, I had clung to Him and found unbelievable deliverance. Now, here I was, almost a year away from August 30, the day Dave had left me, and I could hardly believe what was taking place in the agony of my heart there alone.

I thought, *God, this is the weakest area of my life at this moment. There is no way that I can walk through the next weeks without You. I have no idea where I will be on the thirtieth day of August, but Lord, wherever I am, would You so completely lift me from the weak area that You will make that day the most memorable day I have ever known! God, You can do it! You have promised victory, and I want to claim it from this minute on!*

The next morning we traveled on west to Whittier, California, where our mission headquarters are located. From there we flew up to San Francisco, where we would meet again with our missionary friends at the San Francisco International Airport and finally board the plane for Japan. We had a wonderful missionary family reunion, visiting friends we had not seen during their year of furlough.

We were not even concerned when the

announcement came that PanAm was having mechanical problems and the flight would be somewhat delayed. Our visiting was so precious. Yet we were glad when at last we were on the plane and bound for Japan. The time on board passed very quickly, and before we knew it Barra, Janel, and I were processing through the immigration line at Tokyo International Airport.

I was startled when, in very nice English, the immigration officer greeted me, "Welcome home, Mrs.!" He didn't know me. I didn't know him. But I smiled deeply to him after such a personal greeting.

Then, for some reason, I looked onto the page that he had just stamped in my passport, and the official mark he had placed there leaped from the page and pierced itself into my heart. *Because of crossing the International Date Line, unbeknown to me, it was now August 31, 1972, and I had lost --completely lost --had even forgotten about--had paid no attention to--the ONE day that I thought might have been my defeat!* I had so given it to Christ days before, that what I thought would be my weak moment was a day of victory I shall never forget. God absolutely took that day off my calendar!

You cannot imagine the strength I have taken from God's showering me with His love that day. And I pray that in the days to come I will have sense enough to recognize the large *and* the small areas of

weakness in my life and not permit myself to have to scream for help when I am in the middle of a difficult area. May I daily have feminine reliance on a God who cares for me, and who is all that I can ever,
 ever need.
   And then some.

New Zealand

DEBBIE GIBSON, OUR FIRST CONVERT

RICHARD APPLEGATE

Richard and Elaine Applegate, with their daughter Bethany, arrived in New Zealand in September 1987 about twelve years after they had committed themselves to missions work. There they were assigned to begin a new church in the Auckland area of Highland Park.

Our specific prayer before we went to New Zealand was to lead neighbors to Christ. Now Debbie Gibson, our next-door neighbor was speaking:

"God caring about ordinary people like me is a new concept in my life. Just a year ago, I'd have laughed if anyone had told me that I'd become a committed Christian and dedicate my business to God."

Debbie had been consumed with a desire to develop a successful sewing business. She had made sacrifices to reach that goal, but couldn't keep up with increasing expenses, the greatest of which was the rising shop rent. Although she didn't know God as her Savior, she cried out in prayer to Him. Unbelievably, a building in a prime location became available. The rent was lower, the building had more space, and the location gave it more visibility to her customers. Debbie felt there was surely an all-powerful God who had heard and answered her prayer.

Debbie's only son Matthew began to attend our Alliance Christian Centre. As Easter approached, she felt that she should not just send him, but go with him to Sunday school and church. There, on Easter Sunday, she listened to a message on "Doubting Thomas."

"I could relate to Thomas," Debbie continued, "as

he was an ordinary person just like me, struggling with doubt, and yet Jesus cared for him. This spoke to my heart and gave me much food for thought."

On the next day, the Applegates sought out Debbie at her home. At that time she made her solid commitment to Christ. Generally it is not likely that a New Zealander would have a deep enough understanding of the Bible or of salvation to make a full commitment to Christ with as little instruction as Debbie had, but with her childhood religious training, her difficulties in her business, and the work of the Holy Spirit in her heart, she responded. I knew God had been working in her life for years, and now I was seeing the answer to my prayers and fasting.

Elaine and I have been blessed and excited about the growth and deep commitment of Debbie. It seems that whenever God teaches her a new lesson, she receives it without question and applies it accordingly.

Debbie could be described as one of the most positive-minded, optimistic persons I have ever met. She was full of energy, working long hours in her business, physically fit, jogging, doing jazzercise, and eating health foods, to which her husband said, "Yeech!" Suddenly, in November 1989 she was not feeling well and went to see a doctor. There she learned that she had leukemia! This was the first time in her life that Debbie had been ill, and now she had to face the possibility of death!

Debbie has now gone into remission, but during this past year she has found what it means to be totally dependent upon Christ. In times of physical suffering, emotional distress, and great uncertainty concerning her future, Debbie called upon the Lord and found that His presence with her was so strong and real that it was as if God were physically there as her rock and place of refuge. Although I had thought that her spiritual growth had been remarkable, now she was growing even faster in the Lord.

Shortly after Debbie had learned that she had leukemia, Dr. David Rambo (C&MA USA president) came for a visit to New Zealand. As Debbie was unable to go hear him speak, I took him to visit and pray with her. After we left, Dr. Rambo remarked to me, "I have seen many believers who have had far more years as a Christian, but who have not yet arrived at the depth of spiritual maturity which I see in Debbie's life." Many of us saw it; God was at work.

Debbie, during her illness, learned to become not self-dependent, but God-dependent. She learned that the Christian life is a "walk" and not a mad dash! With her responsibilities as mother, wife, businesswoman--everything was hurry, hurry, hurry. She now learned that hurry equals death to prayer. As she lay in bed for days on end, she found great blessings in personal communion with the Lord. She learned about priorities from God's viewpoint. Her personal relationship with the Lord was becoming priority number one in her life.

Debbie has seen her parents come into a relationship with Christ which they had not known before. When her father died recently, what a joy and relief it was to her and her mother to know that he went to be with the Lord.

Debbie concludes: "Dozens of people come through my shop daily, and I ask God to show me ways that I can be useful to Him and share His Word. I have so much yet to learn, but I am eager to lead people to God. He may use me in mighty ways or ordinary ways, but He uses me just the way I am."

We praise God for Debbie, our first adult convert in New Zealand.

Papua New Guinea

GOD'S FAITHFULNESS IN PAPUA NEW GUINEA

MARK HEPNER

Mark and Carol Hepner, along with their three children, serve with Wycliffe Bible Translators and the Summer Institute of Linguistics in Papua New Guinea. Their work involves Bible translation (Mark and Genesis have been published) and linguistic research and literacy efforts.

One day while sitting in our house in a village of Bargam, we noticed a number of people running to a house not far away. We followed to see what was happening. As we drew near, we heard a man calling in a loud voice, "PAYNOR! PAY! O PAYNOR!" When we arrived, we found Manuk holding his little daughter Paynor and shouting her name into her ear over and over again.

Paynor was obviously very sick. Her breathing was labored, and she seemed to be in a state of semi-consciousness. It soon became clear that Paynor had malaria and a high fever. To make matters worse, her mother had wrapped her in a cloth and put her into her net bag. We believed that Paynor's fever had gotten so high that she had started to have convulsions. We knew just what to do--unwrap her, cool her off, and give her aspirin for her fever and malaria medicine to combat the malaria.

But Paynor's parents had a very different understanding of her problem. They knew only that her spirit was trying to leave her body and that she was dying. Why else would she be going unconscious? Naturally, the most appropriate treatment was to attempt to call her spirit back.

What should we do? Grab her and say, "Don't be so silly!" and quickly give her the medicine, right?

Thankfully the Lord gave us the presence of mind to act differently. First, we unwrapped Paynor and prayed and asked God to help her and preserve her life. That is, we dealt with the spiritual problem first. Then we administered the medicine. We thank the Lord that He was with us and helped us to take advantage of an opportunity to administer medicine for the spirit as well as for the body.

You've probably already sensed that living in a Bargam village is very different from our normal life in the States. Trying to see the world through Bargam eyes and communicate clearly using Bargam words and means of expression is very challenging, to say the least. Often we have found ourselves placed in situations in which we have had to rely on the Lord for wisdom to know how to act. We have frequently found encouragement from His Word. The promise "Remember, I am with you always, even to the end of the world," more than any other, has sustained and encouraged us during our time in Papua New Guinea, even though sometimes the work is terribly frustrating.

Early in December of 1989, I found myself alone in the village lying in bed with what I thought was malaria. I had been to Karkar Island for a short visit and had come down with a fever while there. That was three days ago; I still had the fever.

I had come back to the village to attend the last meeting for the year of the Bargam language committee. Now I was too sick to sit in on the meeting, but I could hear some of the words. At one point I heard a very loud voice saying, "You're cutting his road! You're cutting his road!"

Later, Joseph, the Bargam co-translator and our best friend in the village, came to the house to tell me about the meeting. He said, "Several of the men are saying that they have worked so hard on the committee that SIL should help them--with a sawmill!" He went on: "They accused me of 'cutting your road.'" This meant that Joseph was blocking me from doing what they thought I had really come to do, that is, bring in all sorts of economic development and the secret to the "good life." Worst of all, not one person had spoken up in Joseph's behalf!

If I had ever felt like quitting, that was the time. Here was the committee who had built a beautiful literacy classroom in the village, had by themselves organized a wonderful dedication of the recently published book of Mark, and were even taking reading books back to their own villages and selling them. I thought they were really getting the idea that the work was theirs and that they needed to get involved and take responsibility for seeing that it was done. Now they were talking as though they expected to be paid back for their efforts--as though they were doing this work for someone else. At the time I felt so sick and disgusted that with very little persuasion I would have locked the door and stepped on the first plane out of the place.

There are, however, many things that encourage us because they show us that God really is at work in the Bargam language program. Early in 1989 we were in the village working on translation. One day Tumuw came in and began watching us. He said nothing--just observed. The next day he came back again. Finally it dawned on me that here was a fellow who was hungry to learn how to read and write. I asked him, "Tumuw, would you like to learn how to read?"

He exclaimed, "Yes!"

I agreed to teach him. It didn't take long for the news to get around that Mark was going to teach Tumuw to read. Soon we had five eager students.

This was the start of our first literacy class in the village.

One of our major goals for our second term was to promote literacy among the Bargam people. Now it was to be a reality. We also had to produce reading materials in the vernacular. We were caught somewhat off-guard by this sudden interest in learning to read and had to scramble to prepare primer lessons for each day's class. We were literally cutting the stencils and printing each day's lesson an hour or less before class began. But Tumuw proved to be a highly motivated student, and despite our lack of experience at teaching literacy, he progressed rapidly. He would carry each lesson around with him for several days in his little woven basket and review it frequently. By the time we had worked our way through the entire alphabet and had taught all the different sounds in Bargam and how they are written, Tumuw had learned to read.

One day, after classes had been going on for awhile, Tumuw came to me and said, "You know, I used to hear God's Word read on Sunday morning, and I felt sad that I couldn't read it for myself. I thought, 'How will I ever be able to read God's Word for myself?' But now I can!" We thank God for the encouragement Tumuw has been to us.

Another exciting thing we have been doing this last term is producing the Gospel readings for the Sunday morning church services. This involves checking the church calendar to get the appropriate Scripture passage, translating it, checking and revising, cutting stencils, and producing 48-50 copies to hand out to the congregation.

It is in this area of the translation program that Joseph has really come into his own. During 1988 and 1989 I worked very closely with him in all the different phases of producing the Sunday readings. But at the beginning of 1990, while we were at Ukarumpa waiting for our daughter Katie to be born, Joseph was on his own. And he didn't disappoint us. Imagine my delight when I met Joseph several months later, and he handed me a stack of Sunday readings which he had produced. He had done the whole job himself! From initial translation to seeing that they were read on Sunday morning. What a thrill to see Joseph making this work his own and taking responsibility to see that it was done.

Joseph is an unusual man--a solid Christian with a real zeal for Bible translation. It hasn't been easy for Joseph, either. He has experienced real persecution for his faith. On more than one occasion he has been the focus of jealousy and resentment in the village. At other times he has had to take a stand when his belief in God has come into conflict with traditional ways of planting gardens or curing sickness. Just the same, he has always stood firm. We thank God for the encouragement Joseph has been to us.

If I were to sum up our eight years of service in Papua New Guinea, I would have to use words like challenging, frustrating, rewarding, and exhausting. But in every situation we have found the promises of God to be true. And Jesus surely spoke the truth when He said, "Remember, I am with you always, even to the end of the world" (Phillips).

LATIN AMERICA

Brazil

GOD'S GREAT GOODNESS

ANN HEMMINGER

Rev. and Mrs. James W. Hemminger (Ann) have been missionaries to Brazil under the C&MA since 1969. Ann relates three incidents of God's great goodness.

Grandma's Bible

One of the sacrifices that missionaries make is to return to visit the graves of loved ones who have gone on to glory while they were on the field.

Jim had been very close to his grandmother; consequently, he was extremely sad when she died shortly before our furlough.

When we arrived in the United States, Jim was given Grandma's Bible. We carefully packed it away in a box of books that we were planning to send to Brazil. After our return to the field, we waited and waited for the arrival of the box of books. Since it had not arrived after several months, we assumed that it was lost. At that time we lived in Curitaba, a city of over 1,000,000 inhabitants.

One day one of our missionaries came to the door of our home, carrying Grandma's Bible. Obviously we were surprised to see him and even more surprised to see what he was carrying. He told us the following story:

A young man from Uruguay was walking down the Ruadas Flores (Street of the Flowers). This is a street for pedestrians only. As he was walking, he noticed a Bible on a park bench, picked it up, and found that it was written in English. Although he was not a believer, he took the Bible to the only evangelical church that he knew, our church, located in the heart of the city of Curitaba. The missionary to whom he gave it recognized it as Jim's and brought it to us.

The other books? They were never found. God cared enough for Jim that He made sure that Grandma's Bible wasn't lost!

The Empty Crucifix

Sedenoe was an Italian lady who lived in our neighborhood. Since she had been reared as a strict Catholic, her whole life revolved around the church. She had been taught to fear the "evangelicals," so she would always cross the street rather than walk in front of the "believers' church."

One day Sedenoe's husband died very suddenly. This experience plunged Sedenoe into the depths of depression; neither the church nor medical knowledge could help her.

Her children were desperate! There seemed to be no hope, so they decided to commit Sedenoe to a mental hospital. The papers were all signed; the date was set for her to be committed. Shortly before the deadline, one of the sons suggested that perhaps the pastor should be invited to come and pray. They figured it could do no harm since their mother was so ill.

Jim and Tom Kyle went to visit the home where Sedenoe was living. They shared with her the good news of salvation. As a result, Sedenoe asked the Lord to come into her heart, and she was totally transformed.

Sedenoe had always worn a crucifix around her neck. One day, to our amazement, she came into the

church wearing the
same crucifix, but with
a change. She had taken the
figure off, and we could
see where the holes
remained. Christ was no longer hanging
on the cross--but now He lived within her heart.

A New Life

Antonieta and Antonio had come to Brazil in search of a better life. They had left their native Chile and moved to Sao Jose dos Campos.

Antonieta had grown up in a home where she was taught to fear God: she believed that if she committed any sin, God would severely punish her. This obsessive fear of God caused her to sink into deep depression.

Antonio was desperate, for during Antonieta's crisis times she was beyond help. Many times as he drove her into town, she would try to open the door of the car, in order to throw herself out on the highway and end her life.

One day she heard about the Lord but didn't receive Him as her Savior. Her condition gradually worsened, and the recommendation was given that she be hospitalized.

Special services had been planned at the church, and the members were encouraged to invite friends and neighbors to attend. Cleusa, a member of the church, loved the Lord, and she yearned to see more and more people accept the Lord as their Savior.

One day as she was going to the bus stop, she saw Antonieta. Cleusa invited her to come to the special services at the church. Both Antonio and Antonieta decided to come, and at the service, they gave their hearts to the Lord. However, the mental problems continued, and occasionally Antonieta had crises of depression. Finally it was decided that she should be committed to a mental hospital.

One day after that I went to see her. What I saw filled my heart with joy. Antonieta, a new believer, was sitting with her open Bible. Around her sat several people listening intently as she shared what God had done in her life. As she shared her testimony with the other patients, God miraculously reached down and healed her.

The next day she returned home, completely whole. Never again did she have to live in fear of God, for now she had come to know Him through His Son, the Lord Jesus Christ.

Chile

BUCKETS OF DIRTY WATER

PATRICIA HALL

William and Patricia Hall have been C&MA missionaries to Chile since 1980. There they have been engaged in evangelistic and Christian education ministries in Santiago.

One of the most beautiful and modern of cities, Santiago, Chile, is located at the base of the rugged, snowcapped Andes Mountains. Little did the founder of this great city know that time after time lives would be lost and property damaged because of the natural flood conditions present. Let me explain.

We were facing another Chilean winter, a time of rain and piercing cold. The Andes would once again be covered with several layers of pure white snow. This particular winter, however, unlike former ones in this place we call "home," would prove to be a difficult and unusual one. We had no idea what lay before us, but God did.

June was the month when rain should begin to fall in Santiago, but very little came. July, usually our rainiest month, began with very little rain as well. Toward the end of the month hard rains came. We were reminded of the days of Noah, only we didn't have an ark. The farmers in the valley needed the moisture. The snows that fall in winter would assure us of water for homes and farms in the dry, desert-like summer.

The rains continued for days. In fact, we received enough rain in those few days to make up the deficit from June and July! Then nature decided to play a trick on us, and the temperatures began to climb. Now, to those of us living at the bottom of a "soup bowl," a dangerous situation was developing. Instead of snow falling in the mountains, more rains came. The snow already present on the peaks began to melt.

The current rains and the melted snow ran like rivers down the slopes of the steep mountains, overloading the city's sewer systems and drainage pipes. Normally placid rivers turned into angry torrents, destroying everything in their paths. Homes were devastated, and the major highway linking Santiago with the southern part of Chile was destroyed in several areas; bridges were swept away. It was not unlike another flood we had experienced while living on the campus of Toccoa Falls College in 1977. God had wisely prepared us to face a similar situation in our adopted country.

While tragedy struck the capital city and surrounding areas, our thoughts turned to our son Jason who had left just two days before to go to the coast with friends from his school. They could not be reached by phone. We knew there were several low-lying areas between them and home. Questions ran through our minds. Are the roads under water? Are the bridges washed out? Even if they made it to Santiago, could they get home? We continued to pray. And God answered in a miraculous way. Yes, the roads were partially submerged, but passable. The bridges were intact. Later, both the roads and bridges were completely destroyed, but God had proved faithful and kept them intact until our travelers arrived home.

Now that our son had been reunited with us, we could concentrate once more on what was happening. The floods came on a Sunday; church had to be canceled because of the tragedy. We were concerned about our congregation. The news reports showed uncontrolled flooding throughout the entire city. We prayed for those we knew and even for those we did not know.

Since it was not unusual to lose water pressure or get muddy water during the rainy season, we kept a constant check on our tap water. Sure enough, the pressure soon diminished and just a fine stream was trickling from the faucets. Immediately we began filling every available container, fearing that our water supply would be cut off. Our fears became a reality a short time later.

In a canyon several miles from our home lies the awe-inspiring Maipu River, the source of water for over one-half of the city of Santiago. The water treatment plant sits on a small plateau to one side of the river. The Maipu began to flow with the force of melted snow and rain and totally washed away the processing plant; this cut off our water supply for more than two weeks.

What were we going to do? God had given us the foresight to put one of our infamous fifty-five gallon drums below a rain spout. Soon the drum was filled to overflowing. (The rain stopped not long after this.) We could last awhile with this supply, but gone was our freedom to wash clothes or dishes, take a bath, or even wash our hair. Just getting a glass of water to drink was going to be a difficult proposition.

We asked God to help us through this time--and He did. There were daily hikes to the fire hydrant with buckets to get water. At least we got to see our neighbors more often, as we had long waits at the hydrants! We also had to make daily trips to the supermarket to buy bottled mineral water. Can you imagine hot tea, or even coffee, with bubbles?

Did you know that there are several different ways to use dirty water? With only one big bucket of water you can wash your clothes, mop your floor, and then flush your toilet! We found new and innovative ways to use water. Some of us even joked about writing a book called 101 Ways to Use Dirty Water! Our one luxury every day was to heat a small amount of water with which to sponge off. Washing hair was a different story. We had never appreciated this gift of water until we were left without it.

What were the lessons God taught us? First, we should never take for granted anything that we have available. Water is a precious commodity, and we will always appreciate it now. Our second lesson was one we already knew--that's the reason that we lived in Chile, but God wanted to reaffirm His purpose in our lives. We were there to give "thirsty" people the "living water." When our tap water was cut off, we had other sources to go to to replenish our supply-- the supermarket and the fire hydrant. But--for those who are thirsty spiritually, there is but one source-- Jesus Christ.

Why tell this story? To let you know that God wisely prepares each one of us to confront difficult situations. He stands by our side, gives wisdom, and provides protection. We lost only our water supply. It could have been our home or even our lives. That flood drew people together; it opened doors to witnessing that might not have been opened by any other means.

God knows what He is doing in allowing nature to release its force. It took buckets of dirty water to see and to be reminded of God's protection and love, and to obtain a valuable, reaffirming object lesson for our lives.

Chile

RADIO HOPE--A SERIES OF MIRACLES

RAY WOERNER

Raymond Woerner (son of "Uncle Gus") and his wife Betty Jean were called to Chile in 1955 as teachers in the C&MA Bible school in Temuco. In 1974 they, with their children, returned to TFC, where Ray worked in the Financial Aid department. In the dam break of 1977, he lost his wife and his daughter Debby. Later he returned to Chile to begin a radio work. He works closely with WRAF, Christian radio station at TFC.

On May 24, 1844, Samuel Morse sent the first telegram between Baltimore and Washington. The message of that telegram was, "Behold what God hath wrought!" One hundred forty-one years later, this is the testimony of radio station HOPE in Temuco, Chile, the southernmost Christian radio station in the western hemisphere, and perhaps in the world. One of our texts for this ministry is Psalm 127:1: "Except the Lord build the house, they labor in vain that build it." The emphasis is on the fact that *the Lord* builds His work.

I want to enumerate a list of miracles that took place to bring Christian radio station HOPE into being. The first miracle, I think, occurred in the spring of 1983. I was given the opportunity, at a banquet in Anderson, South Carolina, to speak about my desire to start a radio station in Chile. At the conclusion of the banquet, I was given a message: "Ray, a lady who heard you had to leave early, but she said to tell you that she was going to send you $100 toward your project.

I wondered, "Is this a sign that I should continue? Is this the Lord's leading?"

The next morning I got a telephone call. The person calling said, "Raymond, I was thinking about that--I'm not going to send you a hundred dollars." (*Well,* I thought, *that was a good idea anyway.*) "I'm going to send you a thousand dollars!" That was a tremendous miracle! I had never been engaged in fund raising, so that offer of a thousand dollars was a tremendous miracle.

The next miracle that took place was the application for the broadcast license. I had returned to Chile in July 1983. We started immediately in applying for a broadcast license as the first Christian radio station. It took us till the end of December to put together all the different documentations that were needed, more than fifty pages. When it was turned in to Telecommunications in Santiago, our application was turned down; there was a mistake in the name of Rev. Rodolfo Campos Porflitt, the director of the station. He was half Dutch, and his name had gone through several changes through the years. On his birth certificate and on the application it was written "Porflilt." For two months we tried to get that "l" changed to a "t." Finally, Rev. Campos went to the head person in Vital Statistics in Santiago, a lady. She said, "Mr. Campos, I'm sorry; only a miracle would change that 'l' to a 't.'" She picked up the pen and crossed the "l," making it a "t." She did the miracle; she probably did not realize that through her, God was performing the miracle.

The next miracle was the actual approval. After the change of that letter, the application was complete. We were told that the approval would take two years. *Don't even think of less than two years,* we were advised. Instead, unbelievably, it took only *seven* months! People couldn't believe it. Again, it was God!

The following miracle was the increasing of the funds. There was the $1000 and a little more, but no great amount. I called Ralph Woerner, my cousin, telling him, "Ralph, I've decided to go back to Chile."

He inquired, "What are you going to do there?"

I answered, "I'm going to teach in the seminary for a while, but my first love and my interest is to see a radio station established in Chile."

"Ray, how much will that cost?"

I hadn't given that much thought, and in my ignorance, I figured, "I don't know, probably about $10,000." Such a novice--a stupid answer. I thought about this a long time, then contacted Ralph again: "Ralph, when you asked me how much it would cost, were you thinking about maybe you'd like to help?"

When he answered, "Yes," I had to write to him that it would cost, not $10,000, but $55,000. Finally, the funds were raised. We were also able to pay $3,500 more for the air shipment.

The next miracle is probably the most outstanding. God used it to show me that it was not Ray, but God whose station this was. We were really concerned as to how $55,000 worth of equipment could enter Chile duty free. It would cost us $35,000 to bring it in. After waiting for five months, I decided to buy the equipment and have it shipped, just launch out, seeing what would happen. In June 1985, I started to work on the application for free importation. When I went to that office, I knew something was wrong; I was met with evasive answers. BUT GOD! Here was the miracle.

A Roman Catholic lady was bringing her little girl to the day school at Rodolfo Campos' church next door to the radio station. It so happened that she went to Santiago the same week I was there about the free importation application. She called Rev. Campos in Temuco, saying, "I don't know why I'm here in Santiago. Could it be that God has sent me to Santiago to help you in any way I can to bring in this equipment duty free?"

Assured that anything she could do would be greatly appreciated, she telephoned Arturo Bulnis, a lawyer friend, a man from the aristocracy, and told him about our problem. He, in turn, called a lawyer in the revenue service who in turn contacted the comptroller's office. A spokesman for the office told him, "We rejected that application for the free importation for the radio station."

At that same hour I was able to contact Mercedes Riesco, and she urged, "You must get on the telephone immediately and call Arturo Bulnis. Here is his number. He'll be in his office only until seven o'clock." It was then about 5:30.

I called him. He reported, "Yes, that application has been denied. But--I have asked them to give you one week to see what can be done." He continued, "I think you'll need these three documents: 1) the Christian and Missionary Alliance at Nyack, New York, donates all this equipment to Radio HOPE, 2) the chairman of the Alliance in Temuco, Chile, accepts this equipment, and 3) the chairman of the field says that all this is true."

By then it was 7:30 P.M. I got on the train to Temuco, and when I arrived, I found Mr. Campos very ill and in bed. I said, "Rodolfo, you have to go to Santiago to sign the papers."

"I'm sick."

"You have to go--we have only one week."

On Sunday evening we boarded the train. The next day we went to the comptroller's office, presented the three documents (all our other papers availed nothing), and by Wednesday we had all the documents in our hands--"Importation Free!"

The sixth miracle was the man who installed the equipment, Mr. Ralph Hooky. He was a friend who had graduated from the school of electronics in the

University of Santiago. People warned me, "This man has never installed an FM stereo station before. He knows ham radio and television--he has a TV repair shop--but an FM stereo station?" However, we had no one else. Amazingly, on September 11, 1985, after he had installed all the delicate equipment, we went on the air! Without a hitch!

Another miracle was the area we could reach from Temuco. The station had only 1000 watts; we thought it could reach only fifteen miles. After we began broadcasting, we received letters from as far away as seventy miles. How could that be? We learned later that if the people living south of Temuco would turn their exterior antenna toward the volcano, they could pick up the signal. If they turned it toward Temuco, they could not hear the broadcast. God had put a repeater there thousands of of years ago so these people could hear the radio station.

The next miracle: this radio station, we thought, was going to reach just into the evangelical group (for many years the missionaries had concentrated on reaching the laboring class, not the upper class). How surprised we were within a short time, to find that every level of society was listening. If you were to call the governor's office and they were busy, they'd put you on hold and over the telephone system you would listen to radio station HOPE. Our program is broadcast over eighty speakers in the hospital; the station is heard in all of the laboratories of a local technical institute.

Since 1985 God has allowed a miraculous expansion of facilities. We now broadcast over three HOPE stations daily: FM Stereo in Temuco and in Ancud, and short wave in Temuco, with a possibility of increasing the wattage to reach into Santiago.

God is at work! The miracles will continue, as He sees fit! All praise to Him! "Behold, what God hath wrought!"

Colombia

ENDEAVORING TO HOLD A STREET MEETING IN BOGOTA

STEVE IRVIN

Arriving in Colombia in 1982, Alliance missionaries Steve and Claudia Irvin engaged in various ministries. Steve taught in the Cali Alliance Seminary, traveled extensively in preaching ministry, and helped develop open-air evangelistic teams and literature for the Cali "Encounter" program. They are now assigned to the Encounter church in Bogota.

Recently we experienced a typical example of the struggles and barriers in urban evangelism in an open-air evangelistic effort in La Plaza de Lourdes-- a park where we had been proclaiming the Gospel for some time. That day will stand out in my mind for the particular challenges it presented.

When we arrived at the park, we were unable to take our accustomed spot because there was a musical group playing nearby, making it impossible to get and hold the attention of any people who might have stopped to listen to us. In public parks and plazas one can find anything from street vendors hawking their merchandise to open-air theatre groups to political proselytizing, and even questionable characters performing acts of "magic" with the purpose of getting a little money. The competition is fierce, yet when the mayor of Bogota lifted the ban against gatherings, we wanted to take advantage the very first day possible. We had been hindered from preaching in the open air because of this restriction that had been imposed as a result of the insecurity and violence of recent days.

Once we found another spot that we considered suitable, we began to set up; however, the wind was blowing so briskly that it was difficult to get the paper for the painting we intended to do correctly in place. Then, for the first time in all the years I have been preaching in the open air, I botched the introductory sketch used to gather a crowd. What an embarrassment!

Fortunately, several people stayed on anyway to hear the young preacher present the Gospel. But our troubles had just begun.

While the young man was preaching, a funeral service began in a Roman Catholic Cathedral behind us. At that moment there appeared a demented woman who was "made up" as best she could do herself. Her legs were painted different colors and her hair was twisted into peculiar braids tied with what seemed to be ribbon she must have seized from some garbage can. She carried a stick which she used both as a cane and a weapon against any who would bother her. In her hands was literature she had somehow secured from the Jehovah's Witnesses. Her scandalous yet pathetic appearance was accentuated infinitely more as she walked between us and the funeral service crying out as a prophetess of doom: "LET THE DEAD BURY THE DEAD." And she continued to mumble some sort of religious diatribes against all who could hear.

What a striking distinction between the sad funeral procession for one in all likelihood gone into eternity without Christ, the mad prophetess and her gawking congregation of bystanders, and a young man preaching the Gospel in the midst of it all. I could only think, *What would Jesus have done in this situation?* Could He not have touched the woman's sick mind and made her well, or raised the dead for His glory, or caused the troublous wind to cease? The sense of helplessness and spiritual questioning was overwhelming.

Still there were people listening to the preacher, and several responded to receive free literature explaining a little more of how one might know eternal life. As we began to speak personally with these people (I had the opportunity to share with some in their early twenties who had paid close attention), a group of four or five "gamines" (street urchins) who had been around the platform during the preaching began to wreak havoc. First they took some of the tracts out of the box where both the literature that we distribute and our paints were kept. Then they tore the painted sermon from the easel; it was promptly propelled by the wind shamelessly into the face of a person who was showing some interest in the message. Finally they succeeded in getting into the paints, and one decided that the box should be a different color.

We took time to share with these children, one of whom has no home at all and survives in the streets. He could not even pronounce the name "Cristo" (Christ). Once again we were engulfed with the feeling of helplessness: how to love, how to minister, how to change, and how to win these children and others for Christ.

I was able to pray with the three young people who stayed with us through the ordeal. I have not seen them since, but this is true with the great majority whom we reach in the open air. We are sowing the seed and trusting that it will bear fruit in their lives and that they will become true obedient disciples of the Lord Jesus through faith in Him.

Colombia

GOD HOLDS UP A FIESTA

DAVID OVERMOYER

David and Shirley Overmoyer have served in many capacities in Colombia since 1965. At present they are in church planting among the upper class in Medellin.

Situation:

Between 1971 and 1974 Shirley and I worked in the Departamento de Cordoba in Northern Colombia, and lived in the city of Monteria. We visited small "pueblos" and "casarios" (small collections of houses) doing evangelism, literature distribution, and lay-training. For us it was exciting and rewarding work but also very tiring because of the poor food and hot climate.

One area of our work was in the Uraba, with its impassable roads and trails during the rainy season. The dry season quickly turned travel into a very dusty experience. During this time the water would be scarce, and for the very poor, having sufficient food was a real concern.

We had worked in this area for more than eighteen months, and several small congregations were being formed, each with a lay elder in charge. Our plan of activity called for an evangelistic campaign for four days in the little town of Carmelo, Uraba. Thursday night the group gathered in from the surrounding area and we began our first service, using a PA system powered by our Landrover battery. It was sufficient for that little town with no electrical power, where little ever happened.

This little village was not very receptive to the Gospel, however, and some opposition was formed. We announced that we would have another service the following evening, Friday, when all the cowboys and woodcutters would be in town to spend their meager pay on women and drink.

What happened:
The neighbors across the dusty street from the home where we were meeting planned to have a big dance and "fiesta" where people could spend all their money. They brought in a big gasoline-powered generator and a very powerful PA system. Their fiesta was to start at 7 P.M., the same time as our service. We were not more than twenty-five yards apart from one side of the dusty street to the other. Their loud music began well before the set time. Our little PA system did not have a chance to be heard.

The Christian believers of that little congregation joined us in prayer, asking God to give us the opportunity to be heard. We finished praying and immediately started up our puny PA. The other group had already been going for a while.

When we started, their equipment had a major breakdown. They worked and worked on it the whole time we were having our service. The woodcutters and cowboys couldn't go to the dance, so they came to the service. Four of them prayed to receive Jesus as their Savior.

After the service we played Christian music until

after 10 P.M. The neighboring fiesta still could not start. We stopped our activities and went to bed in our hammocks. About fifteen minutes later the fiesta began and went on all night.

Recognizing a real spiritual power struggle that night, the people in that pueblo were saying the next day that it was not possible to go against the prayers of the evangelical Christians.

Ecuador

THE FIFTH GRADERS' SECRET

MILTON BROWN

In 1963 Milton and Pat Brown were appointed to Ecuador, where they pastored the church at Latacunga for two years. Called to be dorm parents at the Alliance Academy, they served there for eighteen years. They have engaged since then in church planting at the Batan church. Rev. Brown became Field Director on June 1, 1991.

The fifth-graders had a secret, and it was going to get them into trouble!

We had been very proud of the six of them, three boys and three girls, all MKs who lived in our Alliance dorm in Quito. They loved the Lord and wanted to do what was right. They were very cooperative; they worked hard. They knew that they had to do their homework after school before they could go out to play, and most of them were on the first-semester honor roll. But something happened after they came back from Christmas vacation.

They'd report to Pat or me after school, and we'd ask them what they had for homework. We learned early that we couldn't ask just one of the boys or girls; we had to check all six, because after we'd get to maybe the third one, he'd say he didn't have any; then the first one would remember, "I have some math to do."

"Don't you have math, too?" we'd ask the third one.

"Oh, I forgot about that."

After we questioned all six, we'd have a good idea of what their assignments were. They'd do their homework and then go out to play.

For three weeks after Christmas vacation,

however, every day they'd come in and exult, "Whoopee, we don't have anything to study!" We'd check them: one, two, three, four, five, six-- everyone agreed: no homework. Some days they'd say, "Oh, we have a few spelling words to learn." One, two, three, four, five, six--that's all they had to do.

I thought, "Oh, boy, this is really great. These kids have either turned into geniuses or the teacher's gotten soft."

One day I was in the teachers' lounge at coffee break, and their teacher approached me. "Milton, I need to talk to you."

"Really, what about?"

"It's about the fifth grade."

"Well, really, what's wrong? Aren't they behaving in school?"

"Oh, yes, they're behaving all right."

"Then, what's wrong?"

She replied, "They're just not doing very well in their school work."

"What? They're not doing well? How can that be?"

"They're not doing their homework, and what little they do is not done properly. Not only that, they're failing."

I was shocked. "How can that be? It's bad enough for parents to send their children away for someone else to take care of--for me, in this case--and then, to have them fail besides. That's tragic!" I continued, "It cannot be. They have brought home only spelling. It's the only homework they've had for three weeks, they said."

She sighed, "That's the only subject they're passing. They're failing everything else, and they're failing with very bad grades. It's not just a matter of 69's or 65's, but they're getting 35's and 40's on their papers and all their other work."

This was serious. And I was upset, to say the least. I checked with Pat, and at the close of lunch that noon, she announced, "We have an announcement: we want to meet with all the fifth-graders in our living room right after school today, because the fifth-graders are in real trouble for having a secret!"

After lunch a girl came to me and stated, "Mr. Brown, my roommate is crying and wants to talk to you."

I went to her room and sure enough, there was Terrilynn crying. I asked, "Honey, what's the matter?"

Of course, she was one of the fifth-graders. She was sobbing and sobbing, so broken she couldn't say what was wrong. I started asking her questions: "Honey, do you have a stomach ache?" All she could do was shake her head.

"Did somebody hurt you? Did you get hit? Did you bump yourself? Did you hurt yourself?" She kept shaking her head.

Finally, after nearly ten minutes of weeping, she cried, "Oh, Mr. Brown, I'm so sorry for being part of the secret!" Then she told me what the secret was.

The three boys had a little soccer team (soccer is a major sport in South America), and they wanted to practice after school so they could win their Saturday games. So they made the three girls comply with their order: the *only* assignment you can bring home from school is spelling. Everything else has to be done in school or forget it!

As I was waiting for the six children to come into our living room that afternoon, I heard Charles tell Terrilynn, "Terrilynn, you better not squeal!"

The six trailed in and sat on the couch and on the floor. They weren't looking at each other or at me. Then I asked, "Kids, what in the world happened?"

At that moment two of the boys, Mark and Charles, blurted, "You know, Mr. Brown, we don't know what's happened to us but we just feel like studying and studying and studying. And we don't even feel like going out to play anymore."

I answered, "Boys, you *are* going to study and study and study." I added, "I can't stand a liar. God can't stand liars. Everyone of you had better tell me the truth--the whole truth!" Since Charles had threatened Terrilynn, I started with him: "Charles *what* has happened?"

Oh, the thrill of having a fifth-grader, knowing that he was in trouble, tell the truth. It was wonderful! All of them agreed that they were sorry for having done this. They cried and broke down and asked us to forgive them, and we prayed. They asked God to forgive them--and promised such a thing would never happen again.

For the next six weeks we worked with them to get their grades above passing. We never had to mistrust them or question their integrity after that experience.

All six of them graduated from the Alliance Academy, a wonderful group of young people. Terrilynn is a missionary here in Ecuador now; one is a missionary in Venezuela; Charles is pastoring two churches in Montana; Mark has been preparing to go to the mission field.

This is the story of six fifth-graders who had a secret, precious kids who grew up and are now serving the Lord for His glory.

Ecuador

GOD'S SUFFICIENCY

TERRILYNN KADLE

Terrilynn Kadle grew up in Ecuador, the daughter of C&MA missionaries. She attended The Alliance Academy in Quito, then came to the States to major in early childhood education. She has been teaching in The Alliance Academy since 1985.

As I look back over my childhood, I have come to realize that my parents were very special people. Bill and Mary Kadle were missionaries to the Quechua Indians in the jungles of Ecuador.

Growing up in the jungles for fifteen years of my life was a great privilege I shall never forget. Traveling down the Napo River with my dad was thrilling. He started many schools down the Napo which are functioning to this day. Eating all the great food that the Indians served was another favorite experience of my childhood. To this day one of my favorite foods is found in the jungle. When I go back to visit, the Indians bring it to me. It thrills them to have a "foreigner" like their food. For many years we took our baths in the nearby river. We had monkeys and parrots as pets, and enjoyed playing with the Quechua children. I remember that my parents struggled to learn the Quechua language; I would rattle it off while playing with my Indian friends.

I learned a great deal from my parents as they poured their lives into the Quechua Indians. These Indians still remember the love and concern my parents showed throughout the years.

When I was six years old, my parents had to send me to The Alliance Academy in Quito, Ecuador, to join other missionary children for my education.

Except for furlough years, I received my elementary and high school training in the Alliance Academy, where I now teach second grade children.

Late one afternoon, September 4, 1972, my sister Sharon and I were asked to come into the dorm parents' (the Milton Browns') living room. We had no idea why we were summoned, but when we walked in, there was the field chairman of the Alliance. Sharon and I looked at each other, a little frightened now. As I listened to him tell us that our father had had a heart attack at Pano and had died, I could not believe it. It was a tremendous shock to me--I had always loved my father dearly--and I cried very hard. Sharon was younger and really did not understand everything that was going on.

As I went to my room to pack some clothes, my mind went back to all the fun times I had had with my dad--I was "his girl." I would really miss him tremendously.

We traveled all night by van to get to Dos Rios, my parents' compound, by morning. The casket for my dad was in the van with us. It was hard to think that he would be placed there.

Mom met us, and we all cried together as a family. The funeral was in Pano where, when my dad was stricken, he had been repairing a house for us to live in for the next four years. At the funeral there were many Indians. I sat in the back of the church watching all the Indians as they wailed. The experience was very hard to go through at the early age of twelve. I had relied on my dad, not my Heavenly Father, as I should have. It was a hard lesson to learn, but the Lord taught me that through tragedy He is always there to put His arms around me and carry me through.

I did not realize that fifteen years later *to the day* the Lord would see fit to take my mother, also, Home to be with Him. I remember kissing her goodbye one afternoon after school as she was going to make a trip to the jungles with some friends. I'd have gone with her if it hadn't been for some teaching responsibilities I had that night. (By now I was teaching at the Academy. My mother had left the jungles several years previously and was head librarian at the school. We had such good fellowship there.)

That evening the director of the Academy came and told me that my mom had fallen and that they were looking for her. The van in which she was riding was stopped by a roadblock of several trucks and cars, and most of the party got out and went down the cobblestone road to see what was happening. On the way back, she had fallen.

The next three or four hours of waiting were the worst I have ever experienced. Finally, at 2 A.M. word was received and Mr. Brown told Mary Beth and me that our mother had died. Mary Beth and I were surrounded with many friends to help share our sorrow.

My brother James and Sharon, who were both in college in the States, flew down the next day. James came without a passport. He was met at the airport in Quito by some men from the U.S. Embassy who were very helpful. My Aunt Ruth (my mom's sister) was able to fly in the following day.

We learned that my mother and a friend were walking very near the edge of the road to avoid the cars that were coming (the road was only slightly over the width of a car or truck). Grass had grown over a small gully that had been washed in the side of the road by earlier rains; my mother stepped on the grass at that particular spot and fell 180 feet straight down to the river's edge.

The funeral was on a Monday and school was canceled for the rest of the day. The memorial service was a great witness of our mother's ministry as the Indians from the jungle sang Quechua songs and paid tributes to her. Music by the student choir and tributes by several field and school missionaries, as well as a message by the field director, spoke to our hearts.

As I look back over the few years since my mom's death, I realize I have learned many things. I have grown to depend more on the Lord for my comfort and strength. It has not been easy, but I praise the Lord that He brought many friends my way to help me during my times of loneliness. It has seemed like a solitary walk at times, but I know the Lord is always there. He has taught me many things through the difficult experiences I have had.

My family has meant so much to me in these past few years. It has been really hard not to see them as much as I'd like to, but I know the Lord wants me here in Quito teaching at the Alliance Academy.

Ecuador

GOD HEALED OUR SON--THROUGH PRAYER

JOHN ROLLINS

After preparation in the States, John and Ruth Rollins were first involved as C&MA missionaries in church planting in Peru. Since 1985 they have been dorm parents in the Alliance Academy in Quito, Ecuador.

The transition from being field missionaries in Peru to dorm parents in Quito was going smoothly. Though Ruth and I missed the wonderful Peruvian Christians, we couldn't help but love the beautiful Ecuadorian mountains, the climate, and the snowcaps. There was so much of God's creation to enjoy. Apart from the natural beauty that surrounded us, we were enjoying a great group of MKs and adjusting to our new responsibilities as dorm parents.

At supper one night in October, 1985, our five-year-old son Jeremy complained, "I don't feel so good." We told him to go upstairs, lie down, and wait for us to see him after the meal. When we checked, he seemed to have a slight fever, but was sleeping.

About midnight, Jeremy came to our room, very hot and feverish. Later, he vomited twice. We tried to cool his fever in the tub, but didn't leave him in long enough to get the fever down. Ruth checked the home medical book, then hazarded, "I think he has something serious. I'll make an appointment with the doctor in the morning."

In the morning Jeremy complained about his legs hurting, as well as his head and neck. When we found the doctor wouldn't be in his office until afternoon, Ruth asked a visiting missionary mother, an RN, to look at Jeremy.

"He's a very sick boy," she warned. "You'd better take him to the hospital immediately."

We bundled him up and took him to the HCJB hospital next door to the school. By this time Jeremy was only semiconscious. His fever was about 104°.

The hospital staff immediately drew blood, then proceeded to cool his fever. A short time later the doctor came and reported, "The blood test shows nothing. I'm afraid," he opined, "that Jeremy has meningitis. We'd better do a spinal tap."

I had heard how painful these were, but Jeremy hardly flinched in his semi-comatose condition.

"If the fluid from the tap is clear and running, that will indicate there's no infection," the doctor informed, "but if it's cloudy and pus-like, there is the distinct possibility of meningitis."

As I held my little boy curled on the table, I watched the fluid ooze out, cloudy and thick. My heart sank as I sensed somewhat the gravity of the situation. What transpired the next week confirmed what I had been taught all my life about the unity of the body of Christ and the power of prayer.

As we admitted Jeremy and went back to the dorm to begin making phone calls, the word spread quickly through the English-speaking community in Quito and people began to pray.

We first called Ruth's missionary parents in Lima, Peru. Eugene and Muriel Kelly assured us that they would spread the news and ask people to pray. Muriel would come to help us. The Salamanca Church of Lima, where we had ministered for nearly two years, formed an all-night prayer vigil.

We then called my parents, who were pastoring in Talladega, Alabama, and were then at the Southern District Prayer Conference. The delegates at once began to pray; pastors would soon return to their churches, organize prayer vigils, and make calls to other family members.

Back at the hospital, the doctor told us that if everything went well, Jeremy would be in the hospital for at least twenty-one days. That seemed like a long time, but we had heard horror stories of longer hospital stays and of kids who had died or been left with serious after-effects from meningitis.

Our God, however, had other plans for Jeremy. His improvement was visible and rapid. Although normally a spinal tap was done every forty-eight hours to check on progress, in Jeremy's case improvement was so marked that there would be only the necessity of a final test. Just eight days after he entered the hospital, the fluid test was done. I watched and expressed my praise to the Lord as the fluid came out clear and runny. The next day, Friday, he was back at the dorm. On Saturday he played soccer with his dorm brothers.

To us, his recovery had been nothing short of God's divine touch on his body through the prayers of His people.

Mom Kelly left for Peru on Saturday. There she was stunned by the news that Bob Carter, her son-in-law, had drowned in Malaysia while saving the life of a teenage girl. Exuberant over the miracle in Jeremy's body, we now had to deal as a family with the loss of one we had grown to love. The prayers of God's people, instrumental in Jeremy's healing, would also be used to support and sustain us and, in particular, Becky, Bob's wife, during the difficult days that lay ahead.

While on tour in the States one year later, I shared what God had done in our lives. In churches where I had never been, I met people who told me that they had prayed for Jeremy and Becky during that difficult time a year before.

Growing up as a PK, I always heard about answers to prayer, the unity of the body of Christ, and the suffering of the whole body when one member suffers; but now I knew firsthand how great a God we serve.

Ecuador

GENUINE FAITH

JOHN MCCARTHY

After teaching for three years at Toccoa Falls Institute, Dr. John McCarthy, with his wife Alma, was called to Ecuador. There he was Director of the Alliance Academy from 1956 to 1965, after which he returned to Toccoa Falls. He is now Vice President for Academic Affairs at TFC.

During my ministry as Director of the Alliance Academy in Quito, Ecuador, I was able to gain the acquaintance of a number of our national believers. Jose, a Salasacan Indian believer, was one who visited our campus quite often. He would ask for a night's lodging in one of our classrooms. The classroom was always a most fascinating place for Jose and his "companeros" who would pass the endless hours looking through the encyclopedias and studying the large world maps.

For his living Jose was a farmer; he also spent much time at his homemade loom weaving very beautiful tapestries of exotic Latin American bird figures. During the late evening hours and in a poorly lighted workplace, he, as a craftsman, would produce some eye-catching designs.

Since radio station HCJB was an attraction for many American tourists and as the Academy was located beside the radio station, Jose could count on making many sales. I well remember one day when he arrived with his fellow worker and an ample supply of tapestries. In coming to my office, he sought help in calling the radio station guest house to inquire if there were visitors from North America who might want to make a good purchase. As Jose introduced me to Antonio, he mentioned that his friend was not yet a believer, but that he was teaching him to weave and was anxious to have him make some sales.

Knowing that Jose was an elder among the believers in Salasaca, I thought it might be well for me to give him some financial and spiritual advice. Since he was an elder in a small struggling Indian church that had a considerable financial need, I advised him to offer his own goods first to our visiting friends from North America so that the tithe could be placed in the church offering. What a good logical Christian plan--sell the Christian believer's goods first, then the unbeliever's goods.

I will never forget his response. Resting his hand on his forehead, he simply replied, "No, we will sell my friend Antonio's tapestries first because as an unbeliever he cannot trust God like me as a believer to sell my tapestries." The simple yet dynamic trust in the Almighty for the meeting of all our daily needs set aside the ill-proven counsel of this missionary. Our national brethren are living examples of evangelical truth.

Ecuador

PLANTING THE BATAN CHURCH

MILTON BROWN

Milton Brown has been involved in the Batan church since the first Bible study. He and his wife Pat are now missionaries to the church.

"If we're not going to start a church and have services on Sunday, I'm not interested in continuing!" These words electrified the air in the Bible study that night.

Arturo Contag was speaking. He and his son Manuel, who owned their own pants or jeans factory, had been instrumental in starting a Bible class two years before. Their desire was to reach out to the middle and upper class people in the Batan area of Quito, professionals and business men, to enable them to serve the Lord.

Now, Arturo had decided, *it's time to expand.* A three-story building, large enough to seat 65 people, was rented and services were begun. After two years the attendance had grown to 101, with offerings about 13,000 sucres, or $350 a month. Rent was about $100 a month. Then the owner wanted the building.

Finally the men found a place that would seat about 110. The asking price was 21,000 sucres a month, more than our total income. The men thought: *We'll dicker with them and get the price down.*

When the owners found that we wanted it for a church, they retorted: "Oh, no, for you evangelicals, you'll have to pay $1000 a month."

The men were discouraged. One day one of them decided: "We must have a meeting. We don't have a pastor; we need a place to meet; we need to think about the future."

Ten key men, of whom I was one, were invited to a supper at the home of one of the men. After eating, they talked: "How much do we get? 13,000 sucres. How much do we need? We should have a pastor and rent a meeting place. A pastor must have a car and a house that's adequate."

"We need 45,000 sucres a month." One of the men went around the group and asked, "How much will you give--and you--and you?" In that meeting the ten men promised 65,000 sucres a month more than they were presently giving in order to meet the need!

That was a miracle! Never before had I met with a group of men in the church who weren't asking how much the mission could pay to help them get started. "We don't want the mission board to help us; we want to do it ourselves."

They finally found a house for 13,000 sucres. For two years we met there and prayed for property on which to build. At last we learned that the municipal government donates property; all the Catholic churches received donated property in different sections of Quito. Ten percent of all property was designated for cultural purposes, but the evangelicals had never gotten any--didn't even know about this provision.

A year and a half passed before the people of the church mustered enough nerve to investigate whether this was a possibility. Although we were saving money, land was very expensive. Donation of property by the city would aid us tremendously.

Manuel became quite discouraged. The city government had taken some of his land to build roads around his factory. He had tried unsuccessfully to have an interview with the mayor. "I want to ask him if I can get property in exchange for what they've taken from me, property that we can use for a church," Manuel explained at a committee meeting, "but he won't even see me. I don't know what to do. I thought the Lord was leading me to do this, that He'd open the door. But," he continued ruefully, "He seems to have closed it. I guess we'll have to look for property to buy."

As Manuel was about to leave his store the following day, a man came in to buy some imported material. After the transaction Manuel aired his problem--trying to get an appointment with the mayor: "We don't know what to do; we need someone who can help us."

"Oh," the customer offered, "I'll take you to him right now. I'm his personal secretary."

When they arrived at his office, the mayor was leaving, but he gave Manuel an appointment for the following day.

The church committee went with Manuel and explained what they wanted. "Why, yes, here's what you need to do," the mayor agreed, and gave them directions.

First, they were to look for municipal property they'd like to have for a church, then visit the civil engineer's office to make their request. This they did. Matters progressed so rapidly that they thought that within three months they'd have the land. It wasn't that easy, though, as certain people in authority opposed us. The paperwork had to be signed by several men in different offices. Often it would be buried and have to be found and placed on top of the desk, where it would be signed and passed on to the next person.

Suddenly, about six months later, all the papers were lost, and nobody, NOBODY, knew where they were. We were discouraged, but kept on praying.

Four months later, the papers surfaced. A famous lawyer who had been working on them had been ill. When he recovered, the papers were found.

At last our request was presented to the municipal government, where it generated a heated argument which centered on this fact: "Look, we've already given the Catholic church ten properties and have promised them three more. What's it going to hurt to give the evangelicals one property?" And so it passed.

That was a miracle! It was the *very first time* that the government had given land for an evangelical church in Quito. It had looked so hopeless; then God intervened!

A building was constructed; then a new sanctuary to seat a thousand people was added. Between five and six hundred people regularly attend services; we have the key church for the Encounter program in Ecuador. We are trusting the Lord to increase our attendance to a thousand; then we can branch off and start new churches that will have an impact on the city of Quito and the country of Ecuador, and even extend to other countries of Latin America. Already church members are in training to form the nucleus for a new church on the main street of the city.

We praise the Lord for His leading, for His miracles, for His goodness, for His blessing!

Ecuador

"WHAT DO YOU THINK ABOUT GOOD WITCHES?"

CONNIE SMITH

In Ecuador since 1977, under the C&MA, Ron and Connie Smith have been engaged in church planting, first in Ambato and now in Quito.

One day near the end of our first term, we heard a knock on our door. When Ron opened it, there stood Gualberto and Rebecca Moncayo. Ron invited them in, and I put on a pot to heat the customary "cafecito" served to guests.

After the normal greetings, Gualberto asked their important question: "What do you evangelical people think about the white witches?"

No, this did not happen in a jungle village. It was in Ambato, the fourth largest city of Ecuador, South America, with a population of more than 120,000. Nor were these inquirers from a savage land. Gualberto was a truck driver and diesel mechanic trained in Texas. Rebecca was one of the head nurses in the Ambato hospital.

As is God's way--the Christmas cookies, English practice times, and conversation about rearing children, theirs and ours, had formed the basis for this couple's confidence in approaching us with such a question. Ron did not yet perceive the reason for this question. But God did.

I listened and prayed as Ron used the Scriptures to explain God's concern for us. He told them: "It's not God's will to use wizards or such ways to guide us or to heal us."

We noticed their countenances fall as we revealed this, but Ron was quick to respond. "Let me show you what God does offer to His children if they need help." Turning to the book of James, he explained the privilege of the believer (James 5:14, 15). Then he shared the gospel of repentance and faith through which one becomes a believer.

Gualberto and Rebecca decided to receive this gift of salvation, the most important decision of their lives. After receiving some words of encouragement, the Moncayos left. However, they had not revealed the need which had prompted the question about "good witches."

The following day found the Montcayos again at our door. We were happy to see them, hoping to reaffirm their decision. Instead, from Rebecca's lips tumbled the reason for their coming: "I have a rare blood disease the doctors cannot cure. My mother was cured of another illness by a "good witch." On our way to the "curandero" yesterday, we felt led to get your opinion. After trusting Jesus as Savior, I want to trust Him for healing, too."

We were more than happy to anoint them and pray for God's healing touch on Rebecca's life. God responded. Within a week Rebecca was completely healed.

The Moncayos began meeting with us regularly to study God's Word and to pray. On Sundays they accompanied us across town to the Ingahuarco Alliance Church where they were baptized along with Maria, a university student who also received the Lord through our ministry in Ficoa, a section of Ambato.

The Lord began to lead us to think about planting a church in the Ficoa neighborhood. This became our mission after our furlough.

With the Moncayos and Maria, we began the Ficoa CMA church. Within the first year the three became twenty and then twenty-five who were the founding members. Gualberto became the treasurer and Rebecca the first president of the women's organization.

After seven years and the ministry of various Ecuadorian and missionary team members, the Ficoa church has an attendance of three hundred on Sundays. The people are participating in a building project to construct a Christian education complex and a sanctuary to seat eight hundred. The Moncayos are still faithful members there, and several of their neighbors and family members have taken the step of faith in Jesucristo.

The Ficoa Alliance Church is already making an impact on the city and province for the glory of God. Ron and I are privileged to serve Him who died for us; that is why we were here to answer the question: "What do you think about good witches?"

Ecuador

MUNCA AND HIS TWO WIVES

DAVID MILLER

Since 1965 David and Marilyn Miller have served the Lord under the C&MA in the jungles of Ecuador, on the coast, and now in Colombia, where they are serving as directors of the radio work **Alianza en Marcha**, *in Cali.*

"Munca, you and your two wives want to *what?* You are now Christians and all three of you *want to be baptized?"*

I really had a theological problem on my hands! Could I baptize a man who was openly living with two women? Should I tell Munca that he had to get rid of one of his wives before I could baptize them? Should I go ahead and baptize the three of them? "Lord," I prayed earnestly, "my anthropology classes at Toccoa Falls College didn't prepare me for this kind of thing!"

For more than four hundred years the world has known of the fierce Auca Indians living on the south side of the Napo River in the northern jungles of Ecuador, South America. Their brave and fierce ambushes are legendary. As a young missionary kid (MK) living in Ecuador, I had grown up listening to hair-raising tales of Auca raids. Their sharp six- to eight-feet long hard chonta wood spears had quickly ended many lives south of the Napo River. Five American missionaries--all friends of mine--had been cruelly speared to death on the banks of the Curaray River while trying to reach the Aucas with the Gospel of Jesus Christ. Grisly killings had also taken place in other parts of the jungle.

Years later, as missionaries with the Christian and Missionary Alliance in Ecuador, my wife Marilyn and I arrived in the Quichua village of Chonta Punta only moments after the body of a Quichua man had been carried into his hut. The two fearsome spears that had violently ended his life were still protruding from his body. As an Alliance missionary living in the jungles, I had experienced many uneasy nights expecting an Auca attack at any minute. This was to be another one of those nights!

The Lord had opened the door for Elisabeth Elliot and Rachel Saint to reach the Tiwaeno group of Aucas with the Gospel only a couple of years after the death of the five missionary men. But other groups of Aucas, like Dabu's feared "Splinter Group," still roamed the jungles, killing wherever they had the chance.

Then suddenly the Lord opened the door for me to visit that "Splinter Group" of Aucas. Munca was among the first to open his heart to Jesus Christ. He was married to two Auca women in keeping with the Auca custom, and soon they, too, opened their hearts to Christ. And now all three wanted to be baptized!

Should I tell Munca that he could have only one wife? I remembered hearing the story of a missionary in Africa who was asked to baptize a man with five wives. The missionary told the man that if he had only one wife, he could be baptized. But with five wives, baptism was impossible. The next day the man came to the missionary and stated, "Missionary, I killed four of my wives and now have only one, just as you wanted. Now I can be baptized!"

I did not want Munca to do something similar. Should I tell him that one of his wives had to go back to her own people? How would her people react to Munca's rejection? Would they take it as an act of war and attack Munca and the other villagers?

After thinking about this problem for several days and praying for wisdom, I decided that indeed Munca and his two wives should be baptized. They were married, after all, according to Auca custom before they accepted Christ. All three wanted to give testimony of what Christ had done in their lives. I did not want any more bloodshed in this Auca village, so one day I called Munca aside and assented, "Munca, I will baptize you and your two wives. But," I carefully explained, "you should not take any more wives."

A huge grin spread unevenly across his broad brown face. His three good teeth shone white in the sunlight as he agreed, "Good, Don David! No more wives. We will now be baptized!"

Mexico

GOD OVERRULES THE POWER OF MAN

RAMON ESPARZA

Ramon and Kate Esparza, while pastoring a church in Brownsville, Texas, felt called to minister in Mexico, Ramon's native land, though he had been reared in Texas. Since 1964 they have engaged in various ministries there.

"Go to Monterrey, Mexico, to plant a church," God directed, and Kate and I hastened to do His bidding.

Monterrey is the third largest city in Mexico. Old parts of the city reveal customs of ancient times, while other parts boast modern architecture and high living conditions. It is home to hundreds of large industries as well as a center of education with several universities.

A survey of the city revealed to us that although there were several evangelical groups working there, large areas of the city were unevangelized. Such was the case in a new section called Unidad Medelo, where thousands of homes were being built.

We located a beautiful piece of property which we decided to purchase. I was directed to a young attorney, a member of the large urban development committee in Monterrey. Surprisingly, my effort to obtain this piece of land met immediately with strong opposition from the attorney. I could hardly believe what I was hearing as he barked, "As long as I am in power, no land will be sold at any price for a Protestant church!"

I realized at once that I was dealing with an individual who was under the control of the prince of this world. At the same time, I was aware of a higher power than that of man. I had no choice but to follow orders as the Lord spoke to me.

For a moment I stopped right on the street of this busy city and talked to the Lord. As I pressed my way through the crowds, I thought, *God, if You called me to be a missionary to my people and to establish a church in this great city, why have we been refused the purchase of property?*

I confess that a battle was raging in my heart. Then the answer came: "Have I not told you that if you believe, you shall see the Glory of God?"

From that time I knew that God was to overrule the power of man. There would be many battles, but God would lead us to victory!

One day as I was out walking, I met a Christian whom I knew and told him our dilemma. He replied, "I know how to solve your problem. Do you have two persons in your church whom you can trust absolutely?"

Immediately there came to mind two devout Christian friends, a man and a woman. "Yes," I replied.

"There are two adjoining lots where you wish to build. Have each person buy one of the lots, then deed it to you. After that, the city cannot stop you from using the property as you will--this time for a church. But," he warned me, "you are taking a chance, the chance the buyers will not deed the lots to you."

I assured him that there would be no problem about that, and proceeded to contact the two. They agreed at once, and the land soon became mine. Building permits were then granted by the city. The property was deeded to the church.

Today a beautiful church stands in Monterrey as a monument to the power of God. In the midst of spiritual darkness, it is a light to the thousands living in this large section of the city. The greatest victory is the fact that here scores of people have come to know and follow Jesus Christ.

We continue to be involved in other church planting ministries where we have seen God work despite many adverse circumstances. I can say with the Psalmist: "He daily loadeth [me] with benefits!"

Peru

GOD RAISED UP A "LAZARUS"

RUTH GOOD

Charles and Ruth Good served the Lord as C&MA missionaries in Peru from 1955 to 1966, at which time the Lord called them to teach at TFC. Charles is now Director of Counseling, Testing, and Job Placement; Ruth has been Head Librarian for 18 years and now is Director of Readers' Services in the library.

Pastoring our first church after language study, we found ourselves all alone in a recently established church in Trujillo on the Pacific north coast of Peru, South America. Trujillo was a traditionally Roman Catholic city of about 80,000 inhabitants, very few of whom were evangelicals. While praying, after reading the story of Mary and Martha, Charles asked God to raise up a "Lazarus" from the dead spiritually to be a witness to His glory. Little did we realize that one lay "dead" near our church.

We passed out tracts stamped with our church address to various people along the streets, among whom was a man who had a hat-cleaning business. David Guzman liked what he read and visited the CMA church located on a main street of the city. He enjoyed the service and returned with his family. Soon the entire family was converted; thus, he became the "Lazarus" that God had raised from the "dead."

Charles wanted someone to go with him on daily house-to-house visitation. Since David Guzman was a national, he understood his culture and was able to relate more clearly the Gospel of Jesus Christ. For several years, leaving his daughter to carry on his business, he and Charles engaged in personal evangelism, knocking on doors and witnessing to the nationals. Their work resulted in many conversions of Roman Catholics and Jehovah's Witnesses and the establishment of two daughter churches. Here is his testimony:

FROM BOOKS TO THE BOOK
(The Testimony of David Guzman, Trujillo, Peru)

After having lived a life of sin, I give God the glory for His great mercy in extending His strong arm to snatch me from the miry pit of sin.

Of my fifty years, forty-two of them were ups and downs. I always looked for happiness, or rather peace of heart. In money I could not find it because it corrupted me all the more. Not in tobacco nor in alcohol to help me forget my troubles was I satisfied. Neither in politics could I obtain peace. In 1932 I became one of the leaders of my political party and dedicated myself to the fight with all my heart. I was pursued without ever being found. But all this excitement did not satisfy me because I realized the injustice and deceit connected with it.

In religion, as a Roman Catholic, I lived far from God because I saw only hypocrisy and corruption. I was discouraged and desperate and wanted to commit suicide. I do not know why I did not, except for the hand of God; but at the moment I planned to take my life, something held me back.

The years passed and I left the capital, Lima, and went to Trujillo where I married my wife. It was in Trujillo, where I now live, that I came to know the Bible and my Lord. How? Some Jehovah's Witnesses came to my house and sold me the book *Let*

God Be True. After examining it, I noticed various numbers in its contents. This aroused my attention and upon asking the significance, I was told that the numbers indicated the chapters and verses of the Bible.

"What is the Bible?" I asked as an ignorant Catholic, whereupon the man answered that it is the Word of God. What? Is it possible that God has a Book so that we can know Him and man? "Bring me this book," I said to the man who sold me the other one. Whereupon, the following day he brought me this Holy Book. Upon reading it, I felt my heart filled with joy because among all the other books that I had read, not one satisfied me as this precious Book that now I had in my hands. I would never let go of this Book, I determined.

I decided to follow this organization which instructed me in the method of selling books, magazines, and pamphlets because I was told that by doing this I was demonstrating my love and dedication to God. This I did, blindly fulfilling their wishes. But I began to doubt and decided to study the Bible without the help of the books. Thanks be to God, I discovered a system of studying my Bible. Alas! I found that there were errors in the teaching of Jehovah's Witnesses. Calling this to the attention of the directors in our area with the idea of helping them, I was deceived again. I was forbidden to read the Bible unless I read it with the help of their books. How terrible! I was following an organization that I thought sincere and true, but it proved to be an enemy of the Bible and an enemy of God! I could not accept it, and told my decision to the organization, whereupon they expelled me, but not without pouring out their curses upon me--curses which God turned into blessings.

Thanks be to God, today my family and I are

Christians saved by the blood of the Lamb. By His grace unmerited in Christ Jesus, I heard the true gospel preached in the Alliance Church, where I now attend with my family. I am happy and praise God. Only He gives true peace and joy in our hearts through His precious promises in His Word. Now I serve the Lord in the church I attend and point men to the true Christ and encourage them to study the Bible for themselves.

--Translated by Mrs. C.W. Good

ELSEWHERE

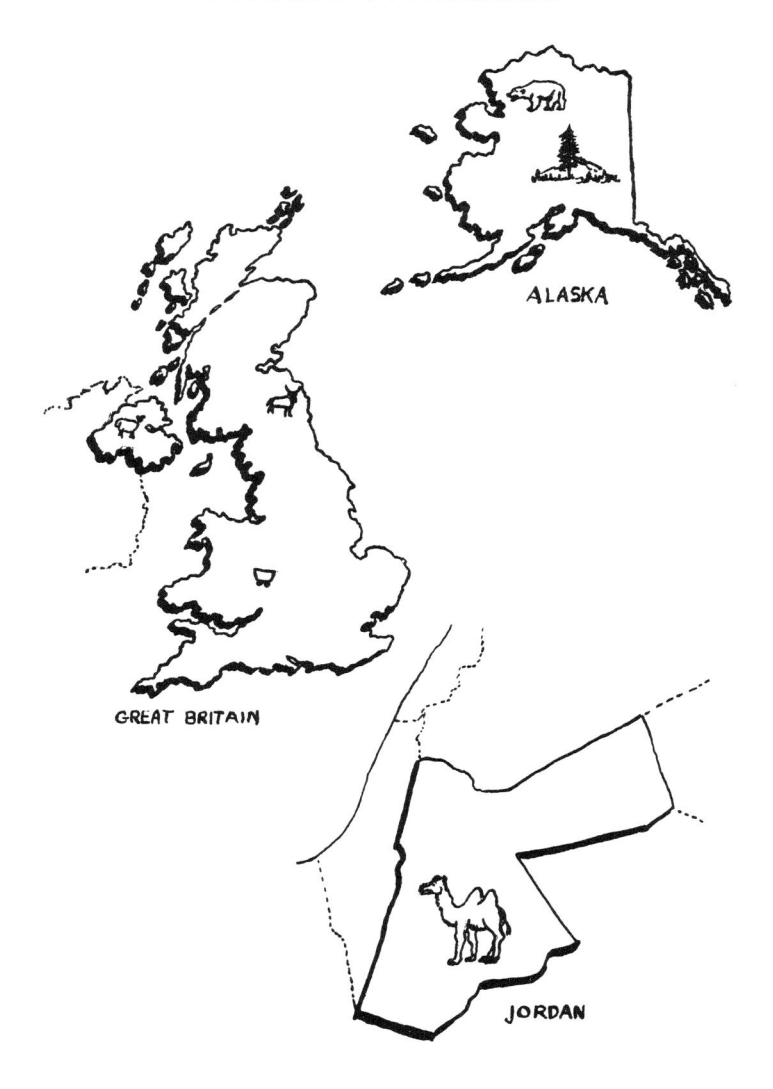

ALASKA

GREAT BRITAIN

JORDAN

Alaska

"HE GOETH BEFORE"

LOUISE COUCHEY

John (Jack) and Louise Couchey had met at Toccoa Falls. They were married in 1958 and given John 10:4 as a special promise: "When He putteth forth His own sheep, He goeth before them." This verse has stood the test of time.

Jack was a starter; God knew this and gave him nine churches in twenty-three years. Jack could envision a Bible study group as a nucleus for a new church. He saw new beginnings possible in churches that had split. He was a counselor--helping hurting churches to rebuild after the loss of a pastor (whether well-loved or seen as a failure). Even in established churches, his "yen" for new beginnings seemed to take over. There he would lead in starting a new ministerial group, or in a coffee-house ministry, or even in beginning a new daughter church.

God would often keep us around just until things really started going smoothly. Then He would point us to other "folds."

The thrill of taking on "The Last Frontier" challenged Jack's special gifts. And by this time I looked forward (with fear and trembling--and expectation) to this ministry. The Shepherd, through the C&MA Extension Director, was leading us to the beautiful "Emerald Isle" of Kodiak, Alaska, where we would work in an affiliated church, while hopefully establishing an outreach into other parts of the state.

Three and a half years later, with a small core group of committed workers, we began a new work in Eagle River, Alaska. In just two years the church was able to call a pastor. By this time Jack was

Extension Director for the state of Alaska, and plans were being made for him to oversee all the churches in Alaska, not just the extension outreaches.

One of our visions, along with a group in Ninilchik (a village 280 miles south of us), was to begin a work there. A ministry to Ninilchik's men, both "sourdoughs" and "cheechakos" (oldtimers and newcomers), native Alaskans and imported Alaskans, fishermen, and those in other occupations, was necessary. While we had lived in Kodiak, we had come in contact with two families--young people who were set on fire for the Lord through a Bible study in which we were involved. These families had since moved to Ninilchik and were burdened for a work there.

After a short time, these couples contacted Jack and me, asking us if we would be willing to make some trips down to Ninilchik to assess the situation, and to see if an Alliance church could be planted there. We prayed; our prayers were definite: that God would build the Christians in Ninilchik, that people would give themselves to the Lord, and that, if it was God's will, Ninilchik would be able to grow with the two evangelical churches that were already there.

With the two core couples, we started a Bible study. When we couldn't get to Ninilchik because of weather or lack of time to travel by car, Jack would take a plane. We tried for a long time to get other people involved, but had little success; yet we knew many people were not attending church anywhere. Finally, in the fall of 1986, after much prayer, we met with the two core couples to ask God what we should do. Finances for this project had been provided; the District was behind us. What *could* we do?

As we met, the Lord began to burden our hearts

to try to reach families. What would interest them? We decided to have a Marriage Seminar. It seems that, no matter where one goes, people are always interested in improving their marriages. Ninilchik was no exception. In answer to the fliers we gave out, twelve couples came. We traveled south 280 miles from above Anchorage every Thursday for about seven weeks, prepared to teach in the evening and to stay the next day for counseling.

One Friday morning after the Bible study, we met with a lady who was having many marriage difficulties. Her husband had not attended the seminar, but Nadine had. That morning we were able to share with her that when she became a member of God's family she could trust God to do the work that He had to do in her family. That day Nadine received Jesus Christ as her Savior. She became our first convert in Ninilchik.

On the way home from one of those meetings, we met an ambulance screaming down the highway. Shortly after arriving home, we received a phone call. The fifteen-year-old daughter of one of our class had been found pinned under her van. We hurriedly drove down to the Anchorage hospital and sat with the family most of the time until Heather died three days later. The family asked Jack if he would be willing to have the funeral service.

On October 18, 1987, we assembled in the school gymnasium, the largest gathering place in town. The building was packed. Probably every family in Ninilchik was represented at Heather's funeral. That day Jack was able, not only to bring comfort to the family, but to preach the Gospel freely. Though we were sad about Heather's passing, we were very much excited that God's Word could be preached here in a way that probably could not have been done otherwise.

The core group met again the following week. This time the burden was that we needed to reach the fathers--the men of Ninilchik. We made a list of twenty-one men for whom we were going to pray until we saw them won to Christ. In addition, a men's evangelical Bible study would be begun. There were four men--two unsaved--at the first meeting. At the third Bible study, a group of men was gathered, waiting for Jack to arrive. The plane to Homer was late, but his friend and prayer partner was there, waiting to pick Jack up and drive the forty miles on to Ninilchik.

Meanwhile, at the Kodiak airport, old friends who had gathered to see Jack off noticed that Ryan Air Flight 103 was being very heavily and improperly loaded. At take-off, the loading errors were evident. The 19-passenger plane lifted about three feet off the ground, then dropped back onto the runway. A second attempt at takeoff was successful. An hour later, as the plane hovered over Homer in a holding pattern, ice formed on the wings. This, plus the heavy load aft of the center of gravity, and the burning off of fuel during flight, caused a loss of control upon landing, and the plane crashed short of the runway, killing seventeen of the twenty-one on board, Jack included.

The Lord never lost control. He fulfilled His promise--"Father, I want those you have given to Me to be with Me where I am, and to see My glory, the glory you have given me . . . before the creation of the world" (John 17:24 NIV). The Shepherd who led us twenty-nine years together has also been faithful in the three years since the accident.

Jack's sensitivity to the Spirit was always evident to those who knew him. He would say, "This is our testing ground for where we shall begin spiritually in eternity." He was known for his generous life. Many times during his lifetime we have reaped from his generous scattering. In his death, the family has reaped in comfort, in prayer support, in financial matters, in wisdom, in peace and safety, and in scores of other ways.

God has brought us through without bitterness or rebellion. On the other hand, all of the family have rededicated themselves to the Lord. God even answered my unspoken question, *How did Jack meet death?* The first man to enter the crushed plane had his attention drawn to one man who appeared to be asleep. As he tried to start CPR, he realized that the man had perished. He testified, "I'll never forget the man's peaceful face as long as I live." Later it was confirmed that he was speaking of Jack. His was a final testimony to God's dying grace for those who have trusted in Him.

As to Ninilchik--we feel that the work we were able to do there was not lost, that God had worked in ways that we had never planned to speak to the people of Ninilchik: through the marriage seminars, through Heather's death and funeral, through the men's Bible studies, and through Jack's death.

Afterwards, one of the Alliance pastors in Alaska asked if he could have a list of the twenty-one men that we were praying for--that he, too, would like to pray for their salvation. (I pray for them regularly.) I know that at least one man who was in the seminars has committed his life to the Lord. Yes, God's work while we ministered there has been a witness that God has used, and I am praying that the churches that are there will begin to grow and flourish and reach the Ninilchiks for eternity.

England

A WRONG TURN--WITH A RIGHT ENDING

MICHELLE TATUM STANFORD

The Lord led T.K. Stanford into Michelle Tatum's life (after she had served several years in Burkina Faso), and they were married. They moved to London as her husband had a burden to work among the Muslims. They settled in a Pakistani-immigrant area where some of their neighbors did not even speak English.

Although England is quite safe for evangelism among Muslims, there is still persecution and ridicule for those who decide to follow Christ. As my new husband and I worked with Muslims there, we heard of many who were subjected to harassment. One man, whom we'll call Mr. A for his safety, told us the following story.

Mr. A chose to become a Christian several months after coming to England. His commitment was strong, even as he faced ridicule and hardship from Muslim co-workers.

One evening he and several Muslim friends were driving to a political rally. As Mr. A drove, his friends directed him. Mistakenly he turned the wrong way down a one-way street. Within minutes a police car followed him and would assuredly give him a traffic ticket.

Mr. A began to pray out loud, "Jesus, protect me and my friends."

His friends laughed and jeered as he prayed.

The London police constable pulled him over to the side of the street. Mr. A pleaded: "Please, sir, do not give me a ticket. This was a mistake. I didn't realize this was a one-way street."

The police constable was insistent: "You were

going the wrong way. Ignorance makes no difference. You get a ticket."

Again Mr. A's friends laughed, quietly this time in the presence of the officer.

Mr. A kept pleading: "Please, sir, this will not happen again."

A second time the constable insisted that he must issue a ticket. And again Mr. A's friends laughed inwardly. The constable pulled out his pad of tickets and a pen. He attempted to write the ticket--but the pen would not write! "What's the matter with this pen? It was all right when I used it a few minutes ago." Puzzled, he tried again, but the pen would not work. Finally he told Mr. A, "Drive on; I won't give you a ticket this time, but this is a warning. Don't let it happen again!" With that, he pocketed the pen that wouldn't write.

Stunned, Mr. A's friends realized that Jesus had answered Mr. A's prayers . . . and the name of the Lord was glorified.

Jordan

FANTASTIC WAS THE WEEK IN JORDAN

NORMAN ALLISON

Norman and Judy Allison, in 1963, began their missionary work under the C&MA in Beirut, Lebanon. They also ministered in Bethlehem, Nadaba, and Amman, Jordan. Dr. Allison is now Director of the School of World Mission at TFC.

Little did I imagine, when I accepted the responsibility of working with a Teen Team of Youth for Christ which would be visiting in Jordan, that it would culminate in meeting and shaking hands with the king, King Hussein of Jordan.

In planning the week's program, we really wanted to use the Team outside the regular church circles as much as possible, for it was felt that their ministry should be basically evangelistic and slanted toward audiences with a knowledge of English.

The team arrived from Beirut on Monday, November 3, 1969. We went to the television station for auditions, then later gathered for an informal meeting. On Tuesday we were to tape a TV program to be aired the following night. As the studio was in use, the director of the program requested the Team to perform in the lobby of the TV station. By the time the Team had practiced the songs they would sing on television, people from all over the station were jamming the lobby and lining the stairs, listening to the Gospel in song.

After recording, the Team went immediately to a 7:30 engagement at the American Community School, where parents of the children had gathered. On Wednesday and on Thursday there were further engagements. The surprise of the day came when I received a message from the American Embassy, stating that King Hussein had seen the Teen Team on TV and would like to have them perform personally for him. Could I confirm that the Team would be able to do this?

"Well, of course!" I replied, slightly shaken.

At six that evening the Team sang at our church on Jebel Amman, then at eight o'clock they performed for a crowd of about 400 people, half of whom were non-Christians. Moving gradually into songs with spiritual meaning and insight, the vivacious young people interspersed the music with clear-cut testimonies of their own life-changing experiences.

Can you imagine such a group applauding each testimony as well as each song? The American Ambassador was present with his family and seemed very well pleased.

Immediately after an encore we rushed to the home of Mr. Zeid Rafai, who was giving a dinner party for King Hussein and his wife, Princess Muna. Mr. Rafai and his wife greeted us as we entered, and moments later the King of Jordan himself walked in and greeted each one of us personally.

We were then taken in and introduced to Princess Muna, as well as to about twenty other guests. The group talked with the King for a few minutes, and then broke up to speak with the other guests.

At about 10:30 we dined on a meal truly "fit for a king," served buffet style by a staff of servants. Following dinner, the Team was asked to perform.

Leading off with a secular number, they soon got down to the real message they were there to convey. In succession they sang, "What the World Needs Now," "Love One Another," "How Do You Love?" "His Love" (a song about the love of God), "Mighty Big Ways," and "More to Life" (a song with a powerful gospel message). The King and the other guests, seated in an L-shaped living room, were very attentive.

By then it was midnight. As the King and his wife prepared to leave, he shook hands with each of us. "You are the kind of ambassadors the US needs to send here!" he complimented the musical group.

After a program for the students at the American Community School the next morning, we had returned to our homes for lunch when a call came from the public relations man at the TV station. He had gifts for each us from the King. Could he bring them over?

Within a few minutes he was at our house. "His Majesty, King Hussein, wishes to present you with a token of his appreciation," he explained, and promptly gave to each of the fellows, including me, gold Longines automatic watches with the royal crown inscribed on the face of the watch and the King's name under the crown. The two girls were given golden peacock brooches with jewels forming the feathers.

Just to meet the King had been an awesome experience for us. And now these lavish personal gifts were completely overwhelming. How wonderful is our gracious Lord, the King of Kings, who allows such events in the lives of His people!

The evening was climaxed with a service in an

independent church in downtown Amman, where the Team sang to between two and three hundred people. At the close of the meeting, six young people openly accepted the Lord, and others were deeply moved.

God is at work in the Arab lands. The things I write above would have seemed utterly impossible before they happened. But God can work when we are ready to trust Him.

Lebanon and Jordan

UNDER FIRE IN AMMAN, JORDAN

NORMAN ALLISON

Norman and Judy Allison were evacuated from Amman, Jordan, in 1967 because of the Six Days' War. Later they returned to Amman where, on June 9, 1970, they again woke to the sounds of fighting.

When we retired Monday night, after packing to go to Beirut the following morning, we had no idea that we would be awakened to three days of bitter fighting between the Jordanian army and the Palestinian Commandos. It seems incredible to write "three days of fighting," for it seemed like a lifetime to Judy and me. Praise God, we were led by God's grace and keeping power through the most terrifying experience of our lives.

TUESDAY--June 9, 1970. We woke at 3 A.M. to the sound of firing all around us. It seemed as if every gun in Jordan was shooting at the same instant. Automatic weapons, large and small, rockets, mortars, or whatever else we had ever heard about, seemed to be all around us. It began with the great blast of sound and continued almost without ceasing until later in the morning, when it became somewhat sporadic. Because of the noise, we could not sleep; we got up at 6 A.M. wondering what to do. When I went outside, bullets whined over my head. I rushed back inside.

We closed our metal shutters, and when bullets came in increasing numbers around our house, we hurried into the hall and sat on the floor. Judy, Mark, Kathy, our four-month-old baby Heather, and I were quite a crowd in the tiny hallway. We had let our food supplies run down since we had planned to leave for Beirut to make plans for the Alliance Youth Conference there. Now that was impossible.

The electricity was off all day; the refrigerator had defrosted. We were using candles.

WEDNESDAY--June 10. We slept well last night in spite of the shooting. It was relatively quiet in comparison to Tuesday night. After a cease-fire was in effect, I drove to the Post Office. Everything was closed, so I went to the Intercontinental Hotel a block from home. Both entrance and exit were guarded by Commandos. I drove by without stopping.

When I arrived home, I found that the US Embassy had called to warn us to stay in the house --and not go near *any* hotel! Commandos from the Popular Front for the Liberation of Palestine, a radical left-wing group, had taken over the hotel and were holding thirty-two hostages, of whom fourteen were Americans!

Major Robert Perry, the military attaché at the US Embassy, had been shot. Two fire bombs had been thrown into his house, then a grenade. While the Perrys were huddling together trying to get dressed (there were three children: two boys and a three-week-old baby), there was a banging at the door. Major Perry opened a glass panel in the door; the Commandos said they wanted to use the house but would not harm anyone. Major Perry, after promising to come out peacefully, went to get his family. At that, they shot him in the back.

We talked by telephone to several friends who told us cars were being confiscated by the Commandos by the hundreds. "Take a part out of the distributor," one advised, "so it won't start." I did this.

Because of shooting in the evening, we all returned to the hall. Several bullets hit our house. We heard many car doors banging about 8 P.M. Despite shooting we went to bed at ten. Once a very loud explosion woke us.

THURSDAY, June 11. The Embassy advised us to stay in our house again today. It is a critical time for the believers. Friends just called and reported that the Commandos came and took their car at gun point. These people had just arrived in Amman and were with C.A.R.E.

I thought I had better check our car again. The window had been knocked open with a rifle butt, and the wires cut and crossed in the switch! Without the missing distributor rotor it could not be started.

Just as we thought things were improving, I noticed a Commando come to our neighbor's place, demand his keys, and drive his car away. In just a few minutes they came for my keys. I gave them the keys and told them the car had been tampered with, the wires cut, and it would not start. While they tried to push it down a hill, I called the Embassy to ask what to do. They said, "Give the part to them if they come back; it's better to lose a car than your life!"

Shortly after, two Commandos came, holding their sub-machine guns. They held up a distributor rotor, and demanded the one out of my car. They put it in, started the car, and drove away in first gear, not knowing enough about driving to change gears! The glove compartment was full of Arabic tracts and an Arabic New Testament. Could this be the reason the Lord allowed the car to be taken? If one of those men came to know Christ, it would be well worth the loss of a car.

The Commandos were now in complete control of Amman. We had no police, army, or any authority to appeal to. It was then that we learned to trust the Lord in a way we had not known before. Just as we were getting ready to go to sleep, a call came from another friend, saying that two American wives had been assaulted by the Commandos and that they were breaking into homes. This was happening in Jebel Amman, in our immediate area.

Nothing could have hit me harder! After three days of huddling in our hallway, sometimes without lights or telephone, trying to take care of the children, and hearing the constant noise of war around us, this was the worst. Every power within me was crying to the Lord to guide.

Our Arab neighbors took Judy into their home without question and asked us to bring the children. We were amazed by their kindness. We were not only inconveniencing them, but putting them to great risk themselves. Since the children were already asleep, I stayed in our home with them, barricading the doors, leaving Judy with the neighbors.

With the children settled, I went into their room

and prayed that the Lord would watch over us in this crisis hour. To Judy came the verse in Isaiah 41:10, "Fear thou not; for I am with thee: be not dismayed; for I am thy God: I will strengthen thee; yea, I will help thee, yea, I will uphold thee with the right hand of my righteousness." At the same time, the Lord spoke to me in the darkness of that terrible night from II Kings 6, "And when the servant of the man of God was risen early, and gone forth, behold, an host compassed them both with horses and chariots. And he answered, 'Fear not; for they that be with us are more than be with them.' And Elisha prayed, and said, 'Lord, I pray thee, open his eyes, that he may see.' And the Lord opened the eyes of the young man; and he saw: and behold, the mountain was full of horses and chariots of fire round about Elisha."

What a wondrous Lord! I cannot say that we were either one without fear, but we both sensed the presence of the Lord in a wonderful new way during the hours of that sleepless night when anything could have happened to us but for Him.

FRIDAY, June 12. We felt that today we must go to Beirut. I called our pastor, asking if he would get transportation for us. He contacted someone who said he was willing to try to get out with Americans if we hired the whole car. With our family we needed this anyway. He agreed to come at 8:30 A.M. Friends warned us, telling us we were foolish to try, but we felt the Lord was leading.

As we drove out through the city of Amman, we saw hundreds of Commandos. There was only one Jordanian soldier with the Commandos at a checkpoint on the edge of the city. This was the only stop we made all the way to the border of Jordan! How many times the many Commandos we saw could have stopped us. Only the Lord knows, for we traveled as if nothing had happened!

We were now safe in Beirut, but without a car and with only a few suitcases that we were able to take when we came out of Jordan. We didn't know whether we would ever see any of our furniture, car, books, clothes, office equipment, etc. again. All were necessary for our work here to continue. Nevertheless, we did know that none of this would have happened unless the Lord had allowed it, and His protecting hand had been upon us in every circumstance . . . Praise His Name!

LATER. Most of our possessions had been dumped into a truck. Although there had been much pilfering, we were able to retrieve many of our things. As to the car, because of my previous association with King Hussein, I contacted him by letter, asking if he could locate my vehicle. Incidentally, I mentioned its value. Shortly thereafter, I received a check for this amount!

Thankfully, we were able to remain in Jordan as missionaries the remainder of our term before returning to the States.

Sunbursts!

Flashes of light in a sin-sick world
Dispelling the clouds of darkness
In far-off places.

Only a few
Of the many missionaries of TFC
Have shared moments of their lives
In these pages.

We salute them--and the many others--
Who have left homes, loved ones, comforts
To make known the Son of God--
The Sun of Eternal Light and Life--
Around the world.

Despite hardships, deprivation, loss--
Privileged have our missionaries been
To tell good tidings
Wherever they were called.

"Sunbursts" have they been
And "sunbursts" will others be
Who follow in their footsteps year by year.
"God keep them faithful to their task;
God keep them pure and free."

--L.M.